Hey Kirk,
Enjoy

THINGS

Inspirational Voices from Canada's Drug Treatment Courts

EDITED BY:

MR. JUSTICE KOFI BARNES

TANYA CONNORS · JOANNE HUMPHREY

ANNIE SCHACHAR · PAULETTE WALKER

 FriesenPress

Suite 300 - 990 Fort St
Victoria, BC, V8V 3K2
Canada

www.friesenpress.com

ISBN
978-1-4602-8649-4 (Hardcover)
978-1-4602-8650-0 (Paperback)
978-1-4602-8651-7 (eBook)

1. SOCIAL SCIENCE, SUBSTANCE ABUSE & ADDICTIONS, DRUG DEPENDENCE

Distributed to the trade by The Ingram Book Company

TABLE OF CONTENTS

The editors wish to thank the Canadian Association of Drug Treatment Court Professionals for sponsoring this endeavor.

WHAT IS A DRUG TREATMENT COURT?

Canadian Association of Drug Treatment Court Professionals (CADTCP). The National representative of Canada's Drug Treatment Courts

A UNIQUE BELND OF JUSTICE AND TREATMENT

Many people who are addicted to drugs commit crimes to support their drug habits. When arrested and sent to jail many return to the life of crime and self-harm because the underlying cause of their criminal behavior the drug addiction, remains untreated. Special Courts called Drug Treatment Courts try to break this cycle.

Drug Treatment Courts are designed to combine the legal process with treatment processes. The primary objective is to achieve the holistic rehabilitation of the drug addicted offender or participant; reduce harm to the individual and society; to enhance the quality of life of the participant; enhance the ability of the participant to make productive contributions to society; save tax payers money and increase public safety.

A Court is a Drug Treatment Court if it has these key components:

- A close partnership between treatment entities and the Court resulting in the creation of a multidisciplinary team;
- A non-adversarial and team approach is adopted;
- Eligible offenders are identified early;
- A comprehensive assessment plan is in place and holistic treatment strategies are implemented. It is a best practice for assessment and treatment strategies to have the capability to identify the applicable issues; provide direct treatment for such issues or have the capability to make referrals to other community partners to facilitate such treatment. It is a best practice to include anti criminal thinking strategies on the menu of holistic rehabilitate interventions;
- Random Urine Testing is utilised to monitor treatment progress;
- Sanctions and Incentives are utilised to encourage program compliance;
- There is ongoing Judicial supervision and one on one interaction between the Judge and program participant;

- Evaluation processes are in place to improve program processes and demonstrate outcomes;
- Interdisciplinary Training among team members is encouraged and implemented;
- Community Partnerships to enhance effectiveness are utilised. It is a best practice to develop linkages with community agencies to facilitate access to holistic wraparound services such as mental health treatment; specialised addiction treatment; housing; continuing education; anti- criminal thinking; parenting; employment etc.
- Case Management strategies to ensure effective delivery and coordination of treatment and court processes are in place;
- Program Flexibility to ensure that the needs of target populations and program participants continue to be served at an optimal level. It is imperative and a best practice for program deliver strategies to account for the significant differences between adults and adolescents;
- After Care processes to promote ongoing success after program completion are in place

Drug Treatment Courts are formed where "Justice and Treatment" intersect. The common objective is the holistic rehabilitation of the individual and the restoration of the human spirit.

FOREWORD

Kofi Barnes

Judge, Ontario Superior Court of Justice
Chair, International Association of Drug Treatment Courts
Chair, Canadian Association of Drug Treatment Courts

The Courage To Overcome

First Drug Treatment Court Sitting

It was 2 p.m. on a Thursday afternoon, someday in 1998. I stood before the Honourable Justice Paul Bentley. Drug Treatment Court was in session in Toronto.

To my immediate left was duty counsel John Zado and treatment counsellors David McIntyre and Bill Robb. Behind us were drug treatment court participants, some family members and curious onlookers. Justice Bentley looked in my direction and gave me the familiar polite nod. In those days, I was the Federal Prosecutor, and the nod signalled to me that it was time to begin calling up the participants.

We spent the afternoon, before court began, discussing each participant. We made recommendations to Justice Bentley on what the next course of action should be, in efforts to enhance the recovery prospects of each participant in their struggle with drug addiction, and in many cases, mental illness, family dysfunction and homelessness.

In our discussions, I was repeatedly reminded of how complex human beings are. It was incredible to see that the same person who has committed a crime, also had a vulnerable side, often characterized by things like addiction, mental illness, and sexual, psychological and physical abuse. It was as if we were artists painting a canvas, each of us with a different brush, and as we shared stories and brought our unique perspectives and experience in law enforcement, criminal justice and community treatment together, a complete picture began to emerge. We often work in silos in our respective fields, so it was incredibly invigorating to work as a team and to learn from each other's work. It was the secret to our success, and an incredibly satisfying experience.

Laura

On cue from Justice Bentley, on that fateful day, I called her name. Laura (not her real name) was a new participant who was still in custody. As she stood up, a court officer whispered in my ear, "she is one of the regulars; there is no way she is going to make *it*. No way."

The "it" he was referring to was the rehabilitation program, known as the Drug Treatment Court method. The method brings together law enforcement, criminal justice and treatment providers with the primary objective of helping people who commit crimes as a result of an addiction to drugs, to end or effectively control their addictions and enable them to live productive lives. Positive outcomes like returning to school, obtaining employment, ending drug use, ceasing criminal behaviour, obtaining safe and secure housing and reconnecting with family, are all part of the "it" the court officer was referring to. In short, "it" was about becoming a productive member of society.

So, Laura was one of the "regulars." She would get high on drugs, preferably crack, but in a pinch, she would use heroin, ecstasy, anything for the "high." Laura's drug habit was expensive. She was unemployed because she was always high, but she managed to support her habit through theft and robbery, or her preferred solution, selling a small piece of crack cocaine for her supplier and dealer, so he would in turn give her a supply of crack cocaine to maintain her high.

From time to time, Laura got arrested, charged, convicted and imprisoned. She even knew some of the police officers by name. When she was released from jail, she would go right back to her old ways and "do it again." Laura was part of a vicious cycle. "Doing it again" for her meant committing a crime, buying drugs, getting high, committing more crimes, and at some point, getting caught. Not to mention, she also suffered from a chronic illness that stemmed from her drug abuse. Because Laura had no family doctor, she often found herself at the emergency department.

Sadly, Laura's situation is not unique. Her addictions arose in a manner that, at the time, seemed most unlikely to me. She was prescribed some medication, an opiate, to help with the pain from a back injury, and somehow, she got hooked. It remains a mystery how Laura transitioned from an opiate addiction to a crack cocaine addiction. My experience in Drug Treatment Court has taught me that the reasons why people try drugs for the first time are as varied as there are people. The reasons range from being curious and trying it out, to masking the pain and torment of mental illness, or some other trauma.

I digress. Returning now to that fateful day in Drug Treatment Court, I looked up and paid attention. I listened as Justice Bentley in a calm, empathic, empowering yet firm voice, spoke to Laura. It struck me how skilled Justice Bentley was at bringing out the best in people. Even in our team meetings, he had a way of making us all feel useful and empowered.

The Honourable Justice Paul Bentley

The Honourable Justice Paul Bentley is the father of Drug Treatment Courts in Canada. After 18 gruelling months of discussions and negotiations with several stakeholders, he established Canada's first Drug Treatment Court in 1998. It was indeed a special feeling to stand before him, on that day in December 1998, when he uttered the words commemorating the first sitting of the Drug Treatment Court in Toronto.

Paul became a most dear friend and until his untimely death in 2012, he was a staunch advocate for Drug Treatment Courts in Canada and around the world. Justice Bentley gave what previously began in the United States as Drug Courts, a unique Canadian flavour known as Drug Treatment Court. Because of his courage in 1998, a resolution between the Canadian criminal justice system and drug addiction treatment began, and thousands of lives have been saved and reclaimed in Canada and abroad because of Paul's vision.

As we began to operationalize Canada's first Drug Treatment Court in Toronto, other cities and towns followed suit, establishing their own courts and producing their own graduates; persons that had successfully reclaimed their lives from the scourges of drug addiction and mental illness. Practitioners in Drug Treatment Courts were filled with a sense of accomplishment, joy and satisfaction, buttressed by the feelings of satisfaction and joy of the successful graduates, their friends and families.

In addition to the fact that each participant's success is directly related to treatment, accountability, holistic rehabilitation, crime prevention and saving taxpayers' money, there were some other special stories unfolding. Those who were not able to obtain the "gold star" of graduation during the specified time period reminded us of the fact that recovery is a process; a life-long process that is specific to each person and highly influenced by one's circumstances. Some were able to reduce their drug use, cease criminal behaviour, obtain employment and return to school within the allocated time period. For others, many more barriers marked their journey to recovery.

I have been involved in Drug Treatment Courts in Canada since Justice Bentley introduced me to the concept in 1997. I am proud to have followed in his footsteps. In 2006, we founded the Durham Drug Treatment and Mental Health Court in Oshawa, Ontario, and in 2012, applying general problem-solving court principles, we established the Youth Community Restoration Court in Toronto, Ontario.

Since that time, I have participated in and watched several Drug Treatment Court-related activities. Through it all, one thing remains clear to me: each participant who decides to begin the process of recovery, who decides to stick with the recovery process and is committed to getting better, demonstrates a sense of courage, a will to overcome, and embodies the resilience of the human spirit.

I have no idea how difficult it is to overcome a drug addiction or how all the underlying factors one may be grappling with, such as mental illness, chronic pain, or psychological and emotional torment, can undermine one's ability to overcome the addiction. But each day in Drug Treatment Court, I was privileged to observe the courage of the participants. I witnessed the good and bad days of trying to overcome an addiction. I watched human beings struggle and fight to overcome their demons, at times when all hope seemed lost. I was fortunate to observe many participants overcome. I observed first-hand the resilience of the human spirit.

I also observed the strength of Drug Treatment Court practitioners, treatment providers and criminal justice actors alike, as they worked hard to encourage, inspire and motivate recovering addicts on their journey to recovery. This was hard work. The twin effort of promoting recovery and maintaining public safety is a difficult balance to achieve, but it is most rewarding. I learned that as we help others, we help ourselves.

Drug Treatment Court graduates and practitioners demonstrate courage, dedication, empathy, compassion and strength. They demonstrate that with perseverance, the human spirit can overcome that which seems insurmountable.

Closing

This book tells some of their stories through pictures, letters, stories and poems. Justice Paul Bentley discussed the idea of this book with Paulette Walker. After Paul's death, we embarked on the journey to make this idea a reality. Our thanks to Paulette Walker, Annie Schachar, Tanya Connors, Joanne Humphrey and all the volunteers and contributors who have worked studiously to make this book possible. I am most grateful to Nana Yanful for her diplomatic but most effective edits of this foreword.

We continue to explore ways of dealing with the issues that arise when mental health and drug addictions result in criminal behaviour, and in so doing, we continue to learn about and explore different ways of increasing our effectiveness in dealing with issues such as drug addiction and mental illness generally. Drug Treatment Courts have demonstrated significant promise in this important journey. The various contributions to this book are all examples of courage, hope and overcoming adversity. It is only fitting that this book be dedicated to the man who started us on the Drug Treatment Court journey, the late Honourable Justice Paul Bentley.

This book is also dedicated to all the tireless individuals who dedicate their lives to helping others overcome the struggles of drug addiction and mental illness and also to those who have the courage to fight to overcome their addiction, by reaching deep within themselves to find the "spark of human resilience" to overcome.

Their stories are truly inspiring. We hope they will inspire you in your own journey, whether through the perils of addiction or some other challenge, and give you hope and courage to overcome.

PEOPLE, PLACES AND THINGS

Inspirational Voices from Canada's Drug Treatment Courts

✮

Annie Schachar

Former Duty Counsel, Toronto Drug Treatment Court

On Behalf Of The Editors

I recently left Toronto for a new job in New York. I'm often asked what I miss most about my previous job as a duty counsel defence lawyer at Legal Aid Ontario. This question always causes me to reflect upon my seven years representing clients in the Toronto Drug Treatment Court.

A "drug treatment court," or "DTC," is a unique type of courtroom that employs a collaborative approach to criminal justice, as opposed to an adversarial approach. Favouring rehabilitation over punishment, teams of judges, prosecutors, defence lawyers and treatment providers work together to guide offenders simultaneously through recovery and the criminal justice system. If a defendant achieves sobriety and follows the rules of the program, he or she will avoid a jail sentence. If he or she breaks the rules of the program, there may be sanctions, such as jail time. As a defence lawyer in DTC, my job was to guard my clients' legal rights and to advocate on their behalf. Part of my strategy for providing successful representation was to get to know each individual on a personal level, so that I could effectively convey their position to the judge and the rest of the DTC team. What I didn't anticipate when I embarked upon this approach was that the more I learned *about* my DTC clients, the more I learned *from* them–lessons in perseverance, humility, and the power of never giving up.

A key concept in recovery therapy is the notion that in order for someone to overcome their addiction, they must change the people, the places, and the things that they associate with their substance use. People living with addiction must realign themselves with new friends, new haunts and new items that exemplify the person they aspire to be. This concept is the inspiration behind the book's title, and can serve as inspiration for anybody looking to make a major change in his or her life.

My clients' journeys, as well as the passion and dedication of the professionals involved in drug treatment courts compelled me to collaborate with Justice Kofi Barnes, Paulette Walker, Joanne Humphrey and Tanya Connor in assembling this book. The five of us worked together to bring the stories of drug court participants and our colleagues to life. We sincerely appreciate the generous contributions of all of the judges, counsellors, lawyers and most especially the DTC participants and alumni who lent their voices to *People, Places and Things*. A special thank you goes to Mahad who shot the cover photo. His photography is an integral part of his recovery and we chose this image because of its position facing upwards.

As you read *People, Places and Things*, I encourage you to appreciate the rawness of the stories and the openness in which they are written. Among these pages, the authors have bared their souls, which is a difficult and brave endeavour. Some of the stories in this book are tales of happy endings; some represent very dark moments. Addiction, as any of life's hardships, is a continuous journey; void of an end-state. These pages contain lessons about the power of resilience, and of the continual value of believing in one's ability to become the person one wants to be. The extremes you will experience as you embrace this collection of stories, poems, and artwork is representative of the extremes that those in recovery endure, and also representative of the extremes experienced by those that support, counsel, and represent people suffering from addiction throughout their recovery.

What do I miss most about my previous job? Without a doubt, my drug treatment court clients. I feel privileged to be able to present their voices to you.

Paulette Walker

Peer Community Worker/Alumni, Toronto Drug Treatment Court

Dear Judge Bentley

Dear Judge Bentley,

Words cannot express how sad I am in my heart to know that you are no longer with us. I wanted to take the time to write a letter to you, just let you know the impact that you have had on my life. The transformation that has happened to me over the last eleven years has been unbelievable. It has been such an amazing journey; I have to pinch myself most days. I thank you so much for putting together such a great program.

Judge Bentley, I remember the first day I met you I was feeling such shame and hopelessness. I had been feeling like there was nothing to live for, and I was thinking, what is the point of going on? I was tired of living and didn't know how to stop the madness. If hell was on earth, then I was living in it. You spoke to me with such compassion, asking me about my family and children. You said that now is the time to stop using drugs. You said that with the support of the Drug Treatment Court team and you, I could do this, that it would not be easy and the team and you would be in my face telling me what to do, where to go and who to see. I believe I said that was what I needed, as I did not have a mind of my own anymore. When you said that if I did use drugs there was no sanction, I did not even know what that meant! That was when I decided that I would never use again, because I had such respect for you I did not want to disappoint you, and for a while that was all I needed in order to stay clean. It was not long after that I started to feel hopeful and feel that maybe I could get my life back.

One of the many opportunities I received was when you came to the cafeteria where I worked to tell me about the United Nations Office on Drugs and Crime conference in Vienna in March 2005 and to ask me if I would tell my story there. I couldn't believe that I could do something like that, but I thought to myself, if you believe I could and took the time to come here to ask me, and then it is possible. That experience opened my heart and mind up to the possibilities of what a difference it makes when people around me are supportive, caring and believe in me even when I don't believe in myself. Today I am so happy with the life I am living. I have the love and respect of my children and family. I have a job I cannot wait to get to each day and I am in college. Thank you, Judge Bentley! Thank you.

Thank you for believing in second chances.

Tanya Connors

Former Court Liaison, Toronto Drug Treatment Court

Reflection

"So what's it like to work in drug treatment court?" I am often asked. "Tell me, what's it really like?"

Ok, here goes, if you really want to know.

Take the undocumented, the lost
The hidden, the forgotten
The disposed, the discarded
Unregistered, neglected
Take the wounded, the bleeding
The scared and the sore
The lonely, the frightened
The despondent, the frozen

Do you have them? Ok, here goes!

We treat, we process
We register, we regulate
We mitigate, we legitimate
We stand beside, we grieve
We walk, run and hold
We acknowledge, we respect
We share, we commend
We talk, and talk and talk some more

We cast spells of good fortune, we wish
We dream, we pray
We hope, and hope some more
We edit and redefine
We always shine a light and we always leave the door open

The clients? Do you want to know what they do?

They do the really, really hard work

Joanne Humphrey

Addiction and Mental Health Counsellor, London Drug Treatment Court
Addiction Services of Thames Valley

Every day I think about how much I love my job and how thankful I am that I get to work with all of you. I love that I get to know your families, best friends and children. I appreciate that you trust me enough to cry in front of me, be angry in my office, and try to make me laugh even when it may be a bad day for you. I've seen your compassion for one another after a tragedy and your frustration when your friends keep making the same mistakes. I love that you tell one another the straight-up truth, but secretly hope you don't hurt each other's feelings. I'm grateful that you replaced the blue pens after slowly stealing mine, that you looked at me and lied but knew I would still believe in you, and that you came back for help even though we recommended you be expelled from the program. I'm acutely aware that life is hard for you, and that sometimes the systems are impossible to navigate, yet you still try. I am thankful that you are still alive after that bad relapse. I can tell that something terrible happened even though you aren't ready to talk about it. I wonder what you really have to deal with after you leave the safety of our agency. I hope that you realize there is beauty in this world, that you are important and that you can be healthier and happier. I trust that you will always do the best you can. You have all made my life a bit more stressful, a lot busier and incredibly rewarding. I am a better counsellor and person for having met you.

Theo

Alumni, Toronto Drug Treatment Court

Show-up

I've got stories. Crack stories, shoplifting stories, getting caught stories, almost getting caught stories. I've got funny stories, sad stories, sex on crack stories, broken bones, and broken dreams. I've got childhood stories, but the story I'm gonna go with is the story that is most helpful to someone looking for a solution. Someone who is full of self-hate because they are killing themselves with addiction. Someone who is hurting family and friends. That's the story I am gonna go with.

I will be a fifty-year-old man in two months. For thirty years out of that fifty, I've been smoking crack. When I did my first toke, I spent all my money on MORE. Then I sold my personal stuff for MORE. Then I stole for MORE. I was trying to stop. I had ideas on how. They just didn't work.

The sad thing about these ideas that didn't work is that I really, really, really wanted to stop, but I just couldn't. I couldn't understand why.

"Couldn't" and "can't" seem to be weak, but I was strong and had will power and I knew what to do. I always believed I knew what I needed to do. I just couldn't. But I knew.

Quickly after I started smoking crack, my days started to look different. Monday through Friday and weekends no longer existed. It was the same day every day. Crack day! Same time, all the time. Time to smoke crack! I was obsessed.

I've lost every apartment I've ever had. Same story. Go to jail. Come out and rebuild and tear everything apart. SABOTAGE.

For twenty to twenty-five years, I haven't stayed out of jail more than three months at a time. Which I thought was pretty good considering I steal everyday-all-day.

I will now give you a clue as to how offside my thinking was.

I didn't consider myself homeless, as I could enter any home up and down Sherbourne Street and Bleeker Street as long as I had a house toke.

If there weren't any drugs left, I would need to go out to get more money, so why live somewhere?

I always loved working out, so when I was off to prison I would say: "Look how lucky I am, I get to work out all morning and then lunch is served to me. Then I get to train all afternoon and then dinner is served. I get a TV cell and when the weatherman says its -32 with snow, again I say, I'm so lucky, who wants to commute in this weather, lucky I am in jail."

Someone once asked me: "What was the best part about jail?" The answer that rolled off my tongue was very true and never to be forgotten. The answer was: "The end of the day." Life is not life when all you want is for it to be over.

I stole so much and sold everything for dope. When I was in jail, another IDEA came: When I get out of jail, why not steal and not do dope. I'll have everything I want and I will be okay.

I got released one more time. I did it. Stole all day. Kept nice clothing and sold some for cash. It was a high. I had a drawer full of nice gear.

I got in touch with my son for the first time in almost nine years. I kept stealing. I loved the items. I like stuff! I was now obsessed with material items.

During this time I started attending 12-step meetings and the Centre for Addiction and Mental Health. I wasn't interested in what either of them offered. I knew better. I knew I just couldn't use. I was okay with everything else, especially stealing.

After a short time, I was back on the pipe. I couldn't see my son and I lost my place and I was back in jail.

PAIN. That's when I felt the worse pain in my heart. Once I was using again and lost visits with my son, lost my place, and lost my freedom, I found something else, and that was HATE. That pain was the greatest gift from G-D as that's what made me want to change.

Who did I HATE? ME.

How much?

I break my leg during a motorcycle accident with a compound fracture. I come out of the hospital a week later with pins and plates in a cast and crutches. I'm in pain but I want crack. I strap the crutches to my back and climb on the motorcycle. Shoplifting with my crutches and falling over in the stores, falling off the motorcycle at red lights as I couldn't hold up my bike with one of my legs in a cast. Then I would go sell the stolen merchandise and then I'd go score the dope. My leg felt like it was just gonna fall off.

As I would come back to my basement apartment that I was being evicting from, I'd be screaming in both pain and anger. Screaming every curse word possible, just shouting out loud at myself. Then I'd enter my place. As I opened the dope on the shelf, I would see my face in the mirror above it. As I looked at myself, I would scream out loud, "What are you looking at, you piece of shit? Don't fucking look at me." I'd turn away. Again I would see my face and scream, "I thought I told you not to fucking look at me." Then I would spit right in the mirror as I looked in my face.

That's sad. That's pain. That's the bitter end. Or is it? I'd open the dope, smoke it and start to masturbate, as sex and crack went hand in hand (no pun intended). Then I'd do this all again. Screaming louder with more self-hate, as my life was falling apart and my leg was falling off.

I went back to jail. When I was in jail I started to pray. I felt uncomfortable to pray as I was desperate and freaking the fuck out. I was in pain. Not just my foot but also my bleeding heart. I wanted my son. I wanted out of this nightmare hell crack addiction that had me. I read a book called *The Purpose Driven Life* when I was at the West Detention Centre. It said G-D loves and welcomes our prayers most when we're in dark times, as one doesn't have the energy to be fake during painful times. Those prayers are authentic. That was all I needed to read. I started to pray and I've never stopped.

I asked the courts to attend the Toronto Drug Treatment Court. I heard in jail it's a revolving door. In and out of jail you will go. Use this program as a trump card to get out of jail people said. They own you, I heard.

What I heard and what I've experienced are two different things. Being accepted into the Toronto Drug Treatment Court, which is facilitated through CAMH as well as the courts, has been the biggest blessing and has changed my life.

I attended a group called SRP (Structured Relapse Prevention). I've never touched another piece of crack or any drug or drink since then.

One of the things I heard was to imagine a line on the left and a line on the right. The line on the left, you're sober. The line on the right, you've got a crack pipe in your mouth. Somewhere in between you can relapse with behaviours. That relapse line on the left shifts to the right, closer to the using side. Another behaviour relapse and again I am getting closer to using crack.

That's the last thing I want. So when I'm at the gym and I have towel service and I'm taking towels home, I know I'm not taking—I'm stealing. Then my brain goes to that SRP line at the left and I know that with those free towels the line is moving to the right. Those are gonna be the most expensive free towels in the world.

I ask G-D to please give me the strength and willingness to be honest, as I'm convinced I'm not okay with relapse behaviour. It'll make me use sooner or later.

Today is June 1st, 2013. I haven't seen a summer since I can remember. I was full of fear I wasn't gonna see this one. But I stayed connected to G-D and I relied on the help of the 12-steps and CAMH, and most importantly, ME! And when I say ME, I mean that I actually love myself for the first time in my life, and that I really deserve my sobriety, and I really deserve my happiness. You can throw any drowning man a life jacket. He doesn't have to grab a hold of it and accept the help. I'm grabbing it. I want it. I'm willing to look at every relapse behaviour and pull that line back to the left before it gets to the using side, which is too close to the point of no return. Prison pain and suffering, and death.

Today my life looks like this:

I've got a place of my own, which I love. I get along well with my landlord. First place I never got kicked out of. I'm working as a personal trainer. I attend 12-step meetings and CAMH. I love life. I am happy. I don't spit in the mirror when I see my face. I want to keep my sobriety. I am grateful. G-D answered my prayers.

Sounds weird, but I thank myself. I'm Proud Of Myself. I've paid back people money and I've cleaned up a lot of the mess I've made over the years.

I'm still cleaning up the mess. The biggest mess is clean, and that was me!!! When I work out and reach a fitness level that I'm really happy with— and of course I worked hard to reach—I need to maintain my fitness routine in order to maintain my fitness results. Same thing goes for my sobriety!!!!!

But how do I maintain my sobriety?

The person who helped me more than anyone was my CAMH therapist, Miguel Disuse.

Miguel: "If I want to exercise and get into shape, how would I get started?"

Theo: "Well, you may wanna join the gym."

Miguel: "So SHOW UP, you're saying I gotta join the gym but I gotta SHOW UP."

(He writes down SHOW UP)

Miguel: "What if you give me nutritional advice and tell me to get on a treadmill for 30 minutes, five times per week, and I eat cake, chips and chocolate and never see the treadmill but I lie to you. Will I burn calories and reach my fitness goals if I lie?"

Theo: "NO!!!!!!"

(Miguel writes down HONESTY)

Miguel: "When I come to the gym, do I need to 'do the work'? Or can I just stand there and talk to people?"

Theo: "Of course you need to do the work."

(Miguel writes down DO THE WORK)

Miguel looks at what he wrote down and says, "Which of the 3 is the *most important*?"

A: show up

B: honesty

C: do the work

Theo: "Do the work!!"

I made a mistake. Miguel said the answer was: Show up!!!!

Why?

You can't "DO THE WORK" if you don't "SHOW UP"

When I "SHOW UP" I can talk about being dishonest & not doing the work.

Today I SHOW UP!!!!

Just for the record, when writing this story my favourite part was writing my name, "Theo." I'm thrilled I've lost my street name, "Coco." I hated him. Today I love Theo and I love life.

G-D, thank you for answering my prayers. I love you with all my heart and soul. Please continue to give me the strength and willingness in order to love myself and my Trevino who I love love love!!!!!!

Daniel L.
Alumni, Toronto Drug Treatment Court

SAND

FLOWING FREELY THROUGH FINGERS
EACH GRAIN AN EMBODIMENT OF PAST PAIN,
FUSED TOGETHER TO CREATE FOUR CORNERS
OF THE FUTURE.

STRONG AND FRAGILE COMBINED
TO DAMAGE MY PSYCHE
TRANSPARENCY A REFLECTION OF
THE HUMAN BEING I AM NOW

THE PERSON I WAS BEFORE
BRITTLE, CRACKED
BUT NEVER SHATTERED, AS I ONCE WAS
GLASS.

Richard O.

Alumni, London Drug Treatment Court

I'd like to first point out that these paintings were directly influenced by my experience just before and during my participation in London Drug Treatment Court. When I was first accepted into the program I was unable to function in any creative endeavor. I credit my time and focus on recovery as part of the creative process. Within a few short weeks I tried playing my guitar, and found I couldn't handle the emotional responses I was going through as a result of many years of co-relating using substances and being creative while under their influence. After I successfully found my own residence it started almost immediately. With a challenge from my primary counselor, Joanne Humphrey, at Addiction services of Thames Valley. She has a background and a university degree in Fine Art, and asked me to do a painting with the concept of "Freedom".

The first two paintings in the series were actually old canvases I already had and decided to alter and add to but in reality they changed and became their own works. First two are the feelings of despair and darkness that came about from my incarceration. Representing my history of overdoes is the "Blue cardiac rhythm monitor line "I painted this symbol because to me it came from the first time I overdosed and upon waking in hospital I saw this image on the machine I was attached to. The blue color is the exact color I saw hours before dying and every object had this colored aura lightly around it This image had haunted me for 24 years and I guess I finally laid a visual to it. Although I had overdosed many times after it was never like that first time I only saw blackness and silence.

The third painting represents the building that Addiction Services of Thames Valley is housed in. With its turquoise panels on the outside facade, which coincidently happened to be the color of my day planner that was given to me for my DTC appointments? The BLUE line following me but being deflected by the building and being swallowed up by the sun above. The sun in all my paintings represents HOPE.

The fourth in the series is MOUNTAIN which is a form of strength of which I began feeling after going the first 60 days in the program clean from any substances. The raging sun above is still trying to process the blue line of death and you can see in one little area a twinkle of the blue remaining. This was but in place for I recognized the fragility of my state although I was determined to put my past life behind me and move to a more normal state of existence, not just abstaining from substances but changing everything.

The fifth in the group represents a mountain of strength with a Star {addiction services symbol} dropping food and nourishment on to a budding new tree.

Sixth one is a fully healthy tree with all the terminologies written on the leaves that I was beginning to embrace and evolve into. Good thing I had all the nourishment to grow strong because the BLUE line comes bolting out of the sun yet shatters from the impact of the tree and disappears. This is how I felt after being abstinent for 9 months

This program, its unique experiences, its focus on honesty, basis on punctuality and public trust has truly changed my life. My socialization with people has done a 180 degree turn which has in itself changed my inner stress which I had no tolerance of processing properly and always used external things to mask my problem. Old solutions have been removed and I have new coping skills and activities that get me through. My creativity was the only thing that hadn't been taken or sold off from myself and I believe it along with a lot of other factors has enabled me to change my True-Self and my inner weaknesses into positional power to carry me farther away from my destructive situations and own behavior than I ever imagined.

Being abstinent for 4 years now, February 3rd, I have got my old spark but it`s temperate with humility, most of the time, and with an outlook on life as this. Do I want or need to be right or do I want to be kind, I am sticking to kindness, helping others, loving my new self and gratefully remembering the help and consideration I received from people who really didn't have to help but found it in their hearts too.

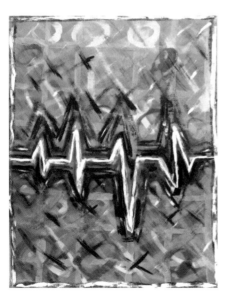
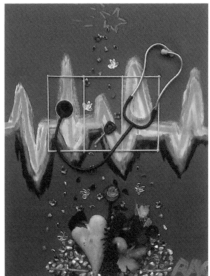

Reo

Participant, Toronto Drug Treatment Court

Listen to my heart
Not enough people listening to broken hearts,
Screaming for love, hearts that couldn't hear,
Disconnected from their inner child,
The child filled with joy, carried in noise pollution
Drowning out the noise of love,
Screaming out for someone to love,
Listen with your heart,
You will hear how much I love you

✡

Judge Mary Hogan
Judge, Toronto Drug Treatment Court

Reflections on My Time in Drug Treatment Court

I was one of the back-up judges for the Court during Justice Bentley's tenure. While I enjoyed my appearances in the Court during that period, I never had the full-on Drug Treatment Court experience.

Following Justice Bentley's very sad passing, I agreed to take on the administration of the Court – a very intimidating task given the legacy and achievements of Justice Bentley.

During the past two years, I have had the pleasure of not only sitting regularly in the Court, but also of being able to participate in the various committees that are part of the Court and also in many of the out-of-court client activities. These include the Friday morning breakfasts, the women's lunches, the barbeques and, of course, the wonderful Holiday Dinner. Paulette Walker, our DTC peer support worker, is the force behind these events, as she is for so many of the client and alumnae activities.

In reflecting on my experiences to date, I find myself constantly amazed by the strength of our clients, the compassion and tenacity of our CAMH partners, and the caring and commitment of all members of our DTC team. We are very much a team, and we respect and work well with each other.

The CAMH team members are incredible – they never give up. Their hard work, compassion and tenacity were recognized by their peers at CAMH this fall when the Toronto Drug Treatment Court CAMH team was the recipient of the Ted Tremain Award. This is a peer nominated award recognizing excellence in service, leadership, commitment and enthusiasm in their work. This award is usually given to individuals, but the team as a whole was nominated. That says a lot about the CAMH Drug Treatment Court team and how they work.

The last two years have been particularly challenging for our DTC program. We have seen the introduction of mandatory minimum sentencing, restrictions on the availability of conditional sentences, and now wait lists to enter the program. The introduction of mandatory minimum sentencing may be part of the reason for our wait list, but definitely not the whole reason. I think the word is out that our program is not all about rules and regulations and abstinence, but about support, compassion, and second and third and further chances.

Lastly, I would like to say a word about our clients. They try so hard under very difficult circumstances. They are what keep me and the Team going. If we have a bad day, it is nothing like the bad days that our clients experience – yet they continue to do the hard work on their road to recovery and graduation from the program. They are amazing.

Drug Treatment Court is an innovative program for people with addictions that partners the Criminal Justice system with the healthcare system. I know Drug Treatment Court makes a difference; but my hope is that one day Drug Treatment Courts will no longer be necessary as we see addiction and all that stems from it treated as a health issue and dealt with solely by the healthcare system, not the Criminal Justice system.

Darren L.

Alumni, Toronto Drug Treatment Court

What Drug Treatment Court Means To Me

Drug Treatment Court has been a saving grace in my life. It came to me by an opportunity of choice and determination. I was, and still am, supported, taught, cared for and most of all...no longer alone. This program has allowed me to continue life even when I felt there was nowhere to turn. I will forever be grateful for this program and for the teams of DTC Kitchener, Ontario and the Toronto DTC. I've said and stand by this: "This program doesn't just change a life...if you want it...it is bringing people together!" Thank you DTC for believing in me and helping me see, "I am worth it!"

Yours truly,

Darren L.
Graduate of Drug Treatment Court Toronto Ontario - July 2012.

☆

Rob R.
Alumni, Edmonton Drug Treatment Court

I am the thief of your children,
I am the destroyer of lives,
I tear families clear apart.
Now take it from me this is only the start.

I am more valuable than diamonds, I am more precious than gold,
the sorrows I bring, they're a sight to behold!

If you need me, remember, I am easily found,
I live all around you, in cities and towns.
I live in the schools with your children around,

I live with the rich and even the poor,
I live on your street or maybe next door.

I am made in a lab, but not as you think, because I can be made anywhere.
My ingredients are found under your sink,

I can be made in a closet or even in the woods
so if this scares you to death it certainly should.

I have hundreds of names but my most commonly called this name that
you gave me, that I love the most, so try to say it out loud, now pay attention, cause my name is Crystal Meth.

Now once you have tried me the truth shall see,
my powers are awesome, try me, you'll see.

Then when you do, you'll never break free,
indulge me just once and I may let you go, then try me again and I'll own
your soul.

I will posses you, you'll cheat, you'll lie,
and you'll do what it takes to get high.

The crimes you will commit for my narcotic charms,
I will soothe and cares you, pull you deep in my arms.

You will lie to your mom, you will lie to your dad,
then steal from your friends and not even feel bad
until the guilt consumes you and then you get mad.

I will make you forgot your principles, your goals, and your cares.
You will be forced to forget the ways you were raised.
I will be your conscience for the rest of the days,
then I will teach you my narcotic ways.

I will turn your faith inside than out, and then leave you with no guidance, direction or help.

I will tear you apart, though you were long-time best friends, mothers
from fathers, then take your kids from their homes,
I will cast them to the streets, laughing as they aimlessly roam.
I will take all that you have or all that you've ever owned.

I will make your wife cheat, then say it out proud,
she will fuck every man you've ever known, even when you're still around.

I will make you watch as she finally goes down,
on your father, your brother, and ¾ of the town.

They have named me this way so you would never have to guess,
I'm called Crank and Jib, Speed and Dust,
so in case you forgot, I'm Crystal Meth.

I will take away your looks and pride;
I will take you from your home and your ride.

I will take and take 'til you have nothing left,
then when I'm finished you will certainly agree
that this time you were lucky I'll certainly bet,
because then next time you need me I'll pleasure you to death.

I will sicken your body, your mind, and your soul;
I'll ravish your body until you lose all control.

I will own your completely, your soul will be mine,
the night terrors I'll give you as you flail in your bed;
the voices you'll hear, my thoughts in your head.

The sweats and shakes and the visions you'll see,
I want you to know these are all gifts from me.

Now it's too late, you know it in your heart,
that you're all mine and you were from the start.
We'll always be together, we'll never be apart.

You'll regret that you tried me, they always do,
but now just remember you came to me, I did not come to you!

You knew this would happen, you were strongly warned;
you challenged my power and chose to be bold.

You could have refused, you could have said no.
If time were reversed , what would you do?

Would you walk away and ignore me, or sacrifice your life to me again?
Well fuck you! You can't and you've taken the first step!

Now understand something: I am Crystal Meth!
I will be with you for years, yes, right to your death!

I am your master and you are my slave,
I will even be with you when you're lying in your grave.

So now that you've been formally introduced to the truth, it's up to you
to decide.
So you know all the things I will do, it's time to decide just what you
will do?

Will you try me or not, the choice is up to you!
Try and remember just what you should do, when me and my family try
to corrupt you.

Jamie M.
Alumni, Calgary Drug Treatment Court

My Recovery Story

My name is Jamie Martin, graduate of the Calgary Drug Treatment Court and former participant who would not have gotten to where I am today were it not for that program. I came from the life of living on the streets for the past eight years, prior to the last year and a half.

It all started when I was about thirteen years of age, and I started running away from home constantly due to not wanting to do as I was told and figuring I would find better acceptance among my peers that I hung around with in the downtown area, who I soon came to acknowledge as my "friends." At that time, whenever I managed to either get back home to my parents, or be brought back against my will, I would steal from home. Be it cigarettes, money or alcohol, I would always be up to no good!

Eventually, as time moved on, and after being told to leave by my mother because of the trouble I was causing, I started getting to know more of the people on the street and getting into the drug scene. I smoked my first marijuana cigarette at the age of fourteen, did my first hit of LSD at the age of fifteen and tried crack cocaine for the first time at the age of eighteen. Throughout this whole time of growing up without really maturing, I was still into getting drunk on alcohol whenever the opportunity presented itself. At the same time, I was, every once in a while, dabbling in criminal activity such as car prowling, petty theft and trespassing (for the purpose of sleep).

After turning nineteen and having abstained from the heavy partying life for a short period of time, I received an inheritance in the range of twenty-four thousand dollars. During this time, I had met a girl who I thought I came to fall in love with. I kept her by my side for a long enough period of time. We had partied a lot together and, at that time, were having what seemed to be "the time of our lives." When the inheritance arrived, I got us a place in Airdrie close to my uncle so I was able to gain employment with him. While residing in Airdrie and spending the entire new-found fortune in a matter of months on drinking and getting high on pretty much a daily basis, the love of my life (at that time!) and I became pregnant with our first child, Justice.

After a time and losing our place in Airdrie (along with my employment), she moved back to Calgary to live with her family while I fell harder into the party scene. I went from drinking and drugging to just plain drugging on cocaine. I lost everything material that I had spent my inheritance on and welcomed the streets back into my life. I went back to the small criminal activities I had come to learn about in the years prior until I had made enough of an impression on my girlfriend's family to be willing to take me in so I could attempt to be a father to our child. Then we got pregnant with our second child, a son. I now thought it was time to step up my game, so I stopped working in the kitchen industry and went back to construction. Roofing was the last form of employment for me prior to this program.

I was doing roofing with a guy who subcontracted a lot of work pretty well year round, so I kept busy. I was making enough to get us by, along with whatever funds my girlfriend was able to milk out of the system. So even though I thought I was the "man," our life was still corrupt with the use of marijuana and me going out drinking whenever I felt like it. Our relationship was off and on for about three years after Justice was born, with us always moving from one place to the next. We were never able to keep a place for more than six months, it seemed. The place we resided together was in the Whitehorn area not far from the station. By this time I was roofing for a different company, still thinking that I was the "man," if you know what I mean! Brought home the bacon, blah, blah!

Anyway, that was the last I was to see of my family for quite some time. After some really bad arguments—me punching holes in walls and her slicing stuff up such as walls—we were arguing pretty bad one day and our son was crying in the hall. I walked up to him to ask what was wrong and he screamed back at me. Being already heated from the arguing with his mother, I wasn't thinking and gave him a smack in the face that later bruised his eye. A couple days later, I came home after work to find a Child Protective Services/Family Services card attached to my wall with the message "call us" written on it. So I called the next day and met with them to see what had happened with my family and was told that the situation was explained to them and they needed to hear my side. After telling them the entire truth, I was charged and arrested for assault on a minor. That got me a sentence of two years probation with one of the conditions being refraining from any communication with my family.

That was the end of my world as I had come to know it. I started giving up hope of ever seeing my kids again and the idea of ever living a normal life. I quit my job soon after falling into the crack scene with a roommate I was living with in the Bridgeland area. We turned that basement suite into a crack-shack, people coming over all the time doing their drugs and whatever, wherever, which eventually led to an eviction due to not paying the rent.

Back to the downtown area I went, learning how to push the stuff on the street while trying not to get myself into too much debt with the China-man! Because my use of drugs outweighed my determination to make money with it, I ended up getting into a small but substantial amount of debt that I couldn't pay back. I didn't contact the person to whom I owed money and he eventually ended up getting killed as a result of being gang affiliated. That was a big deterrent for me - to stay away from getting myself involved in any gang activity. With that in mind, I proceeded to get into the life of panhandling and found I was pretty good at making the hearts of society bleed along with their wallets or loose change. I also found myself spending obscene amounts of unearned funds on my addiction. It wasn't long before I was introduced to the way of "earning" money as a squeegee kid. I started washing car windows with others at traffic intersections, primarily around the McDonalds on 17th Avenue s.w. This seemed to be the place where lots of money could be made through squeegeeing, panhandling and hooking people up with drugs. Eventually, when police presence had become an interference with what we tried to accomplish in that area, I learned through others how to do things such as break into coin-operated devices and, using high-powered magnets, extract the coins in short periods of time. With this newfound knowledge, along with the know-how of entering buildings, I went from doing newspaper boxes to laundry machines. During this time, I had also been shown how to steal Honda Civics (later models). The progression of my addiction eventually held no boundaries for me. That entailed less and less care for myself as well as society. I was being sent to jail off and on through this entire time, to which I had become accustomed, and by the same token, had met more people that taught me how to do more crimes, and eventually I just didn't care how I got money or drugs as long as I didn't get caught. This led to some high-speed pursuits with police and other such things for which I feel I am very fortunate nobody was ever physically harmed.

My last incidents involving any drugs, alcohol or crime consisted of a break and enter on a laundromat and dangerous driving involving evading the Calgary Police Service. October 17th, 2011, was the day I said I was done. It had become my rescue date! My lawyer told me I was facing up to two years in jail and that was something I did not want to do. I enjoyed my freedom. I asked about the Drug Treatment Court Program, at first as a way out of jail, but once I started putting pen to paper and seeing the things I had to live for, I figured it was time to give change a try. I was accepted in the CDTC program and, as a result, sent to Simon House Recovery Centre for men.

At first it wasn't easy, being told all these things I needed to commit to such as chores, shaving every morning and "shut up and listen!" Because I didn't want to go back to jail, I put on the façade of doing as I was told the first little while; I wasn't listening too well due to the nature of not being comfortable with this new way of living. I was used to doing what I wanted, when I wanted, wherever I wanted and didn't ever enjoy taking BS from anyone. And that's what I always perceived it as—BS. Then I heard in a group session one day when I was starting to listen that I had no idea how to live my own life the way it was meant to be lived and knew nothing about how to stay clean and sober while at the same time being able to be happy with my life. This really hit home for me and I decided then that it was time to start letting go of the way I ran my life and just let it happen. I went through the first five steps they talk about in Alcoholics Anonymous in the House. While going to these meetings and getting introduced to a wide variety of others who had similar experiences to mine, I found myself becoming more and more comfortable going to these rooms and learning that I wasn't alone anymore and that there are people outside the walls of jails and institutions that could help when I am struggling.

After getting a sponsor in the program of AA, getting a Home Group and getting myself involved in the fellowship, I finished the group portion of treatment at Simon House and proceeded to seek out employment. My first job was attained through a fellow who also resided at the House and I found myself working in a kitchen at the concession of Bingo Barn. I held this job for about five months when another opportunity arose for me to make better money working for a company called Sealtech Restorations doing asbestos abatement. Since acquiring this job, I have been able to hold onto it now for a little over nine months. While working for the company and still residing at Simon House, I have been able to open a bank account and pro-ceeded to save money for my future, which is looking brighter every day. I have gone through Phase 2 and into Phase 3 at the House and had the opportunity to learn how to sponsor others in the program of AA. What used to be a hopeless state of mind when it came to thinking I would never see my family again has grown into a hopeful one, for I have, as of the last six months, been visiting my two children on a regular basis and speaking with my parents again, as well. As of April 8th, 2013, I have been in a relationship with a wonderful woman by the name of Dawn for a year, and we'll be moving in together as of May 1st, 2013. My life today has made a complete 180! I no longer have to resort to mind-altering substances to numb my feelings, because I have been shown how to face them and deal with them properly. I have relation-ships, not just with a power greater than myself, whom I choose to call God, but with friends and family as well. I have been able to keep up with bills, pay off old debts, and have been given a key and position as General Institutions Representative at my AA Home Group. I have trust in others and others trust in me in ways I never thought possible.

I am becoming more responsible each and every day, and it's all a result of putting recovery first and foremost in my life. I wouldn't trade the worst days I have today for the best ones I had in my using days. I thank God for where I am at in life today because I have been shown that I deserve to live.

☆

Linda Cartain
Therapist, Toronto Drug Treatment Court

Graduation Speech for my Client Elaine H. (May 31, 2012)

Good afternoon, Your Honour, Crown, Probation, Duty Counsel, Treatment, Family, Friends and Clients. We are here today to celebrate the graduation of Robert and Elaine H. This is a very special day in Drug Treatment Court, as two clients have fulfilled their obligations to themselves and the DTC program.

I would now like to give you a bit of history around Elaine's journey through DTC. When Elaine entered the program in November 2009, she was living in the Women's Residential shelter because she was homeless. At that point she started to attend the preparation group at the Russell Street CAMH location. Her initial therapist was Kristal. As I read through Elaine's file preparing for today, I noticed a case note that Kristal had written on November 16, 2009. Elaine, you told her at that time that you considered your miracle to be having your own apartment, getting a dog and regaining the respect of your family back. Just so you are aware, sitting here today, your miracle has been realized. You have everything back that you wanted when you first came into DTC.

Elaine remained in the prep group until February 9, 2010, when she entered the three week structured relapse prevention group at our White Squirrel Way location. In mid-February she moved into her own apartment. She completed the SRP group and started attending the maintenance group in March 2010. Elaine also worked with Joanne Short, another therapist in DTC, until she was assigned to my caseload in December 2010. Elaine continued to attend the maintenance group until September 2011, when she made the decision to be admitted into the women's program at WSW. She remained there until mid-October and then returned to maintenance. In March 2012, she began attending the Continuing Care Group at WSW, which she is attending to this day.

That was a bit about her journey through DTC! Elaine came to us later in life, as I am happy to say that she was a late bloomer with her crack use. Prior to that, much of Elaine's life was about looking after others. She was taught that from a very early age. She coped with life that way. It kept her mind off herself. Her upbringing was very unhealthy and she was hurt in so many ways. When her husband died a few years back, Elaine found herself on her own with no one to focus on. The pain would not go away. She started to use crack and that added more pain on her plate. Not only did she have her history to deal with, but now she also had an active addiction that took her places she never thought she would go to.

Elaine has been in this program for quite a while. Most of that is due to health issues that have needed to be addressed as she has gone along. She has continued to express to me the love she has for her daughter and her grandchildren. She is very close to her grandson. I believe both of them are here today – I just want to tell you that you have been a great motivator in Elaine's life. She wants to be well and healthy so she can enjoy being with her family once again.

Elaine, you have a marvellous heart! I have thoroughly enjoyed watching you grow and change. Remember this is only the beginning. Keep up with your groups and don't disengage from treatment.

Tom B.

Participant, London Drug Treatment Court

When I think about it nowadays, I guess I have been fighting addiction my whole life. But I guess I never realized it until a couple of years back when I was in a Treatment Centre reading the Narcotics Anonymous book that said "my best thinking put me right here." I would never have thought that I would have ever gone to a treatment center. But I was starting to hit rock bottom. I was no longer talking to my family or old friends that weren't doing drugs. I no longer had my business; I had lost everything I owned twice and even lost my pet of seventeen years. But for me, jail was my rock bottom. My lost time in jail was no longer acceptable, and this time I was looking at penitentiary time of over two years. In just six or seven years I had amassed over one hundred convictions, mostly all for stealing so I could afford my addiction. I don't mind telling anyone that at the age of fifty years old I was terrified of doing two years in jail. Doing three months, twenty-one days, forty-four days, two months, one year, four months, etcetera - they were all acceptable. The price I had to pay to afford my addiction. I was now at rock bottom. We all have our rock bottoms, and to me, going to the pen was it. Then my lawyer, who I will always thank for saving me and getting me into Drug Treatment Court, told me there was a way I could get out of jail. I would have done anything. Now I am in Drug Treatment Court, and off drugs for over 120 days on the street. I have never felt better and can see clearly, down the road, running my own business again and living a straight life. I have a solid relationship with someone who is also off drugs and life is looking good. I go to my addiction courses and take my drug tests, which are always negative to drugs, which always makes me feel good. All I can say is you really, really have to want to change your life, but I'll tell anyone who wants to listen, your life will change for the better once you stay off drugs. It does get better. I'm happy almost every day. Drug Treatment Court has put stability and meaning back into my life.

Peter Lye
Alumni, Toronto Drug Treatment Court

Never Too Late
10th anniversary address at Old City Hall Courthouse

I'm glad we are here where I watched my first graduation at Toronto Drug Treatment Court. That was when I first believed I would make it.

We anchor or ground ourselves in a firm "take care of number one," or like my mother, in the humanism of Bertrand Russell. But many ground themselves in spirituality.

Anyways, once you're grounded you have a way of sorting out morality and relationships. Much becomes possible. Our example is achieving sobriety; much easier with your rationale and a purpose (graduation). I entered recovery under persuasion from authority, family and self. I slowly made progress, but became amazed and thrilled by what was happening in my fifties yet – beyond graduation. I had equated the mental self-examination and understanding that you need to turning over rocks in a weedy garden; something to be avoided and postponed. Instead of crawly things, I discovered near-magical sequences and events in my past that I had suppressed. And new things happened to me as I struggled with Drug Treatment Court. In sum, they signified an all-pervasive force for good within ourselves and events.

Indeed I was amazed that an ostensibly adversarial process could be so supportive. As it went on, I was inspired to continue my volunteer work, encouraging housing as the major piece in recovery and the understanding of this issue.

A week ago, I spoke to a class in a school of social work and participated in a United Way project called SHIFT – an eight-month, ongoing think-tank on homelessness. With a music group, I play at community events where I grew up. They seem glad to see me.

Now I'm doing what I was doing at eighteen, before I ever tried drugs. But because of quiet time, I've learned to appreciate, and because of guidance, I have acquired what was lacking forty years ago: some kind of spiritual grounding. Each must divine his own. It's never too late. I know this because I discovered more than sobriety through my work with Drug Treatment Court and the alumni; I found a purpose.

Thank you.

Drug Treatment Court Song

Verse 1
Flat out on the rug, on my favourite drug.
Flat out on the rug, on my favourite drug.
When the police came crashing through the door
Then I knew I would need my day in court.
By my mother bailed, of a lawyer I availed.

She had good news to report:
Something about drug treatment court.

Chorus
Drug treatment court, drug treatment court,
Good news to report!
You can't lose at all in drug treatment court

Drug treatment court,
Whatever you shoot, smoke or snort,
You won't use at all after drug treatment court.

Verse 2
After a little romp, treatment started prompt.
And I begged to be let into the court.
Judge said yes, spanked us, and sent us on our course.

Chorus
Drug treatment court, drug treatment court,
Good news to report!
You can't lose at all in drug treatment court

Drug treatment court,
Whatever you shoot, smoke or snort,
You won't use at all after drug treatment court.

Verse 3
Now we are free for good,
Back in our ol` hood,
That policeman is our new neighbour,
But that is what drug court is for!
Now we work and play, juniors on the way,
We are high on God, clean air and sport!

All because of drug treatment court.

Remembering Peter Lye

MAY 21, 2014

Peter Lye was a graduate and founding Alumni of the Toronto Drug Treatment Court Program. His song "Drug Treatment Court" has been performed and brought smiles to local Toronto audience's as well national and international friends of Drug Treatment Courts as it has performed at the National Drug Treatment Court conference.

Peter was also an active and founding member of The Dream Team, a Toronto based advocacy group, working to secure safe, affordable, supportive housing. Peter's energy, enthusiasm and humor are greatly missed.

☆

Deany Peters
Community Development Worker, Toronto

Address from Memorial Event for Justice Paul Bentley

On behalf of the Toronto Drug Treatment Court, Community Advisory Committee, I share these thoughts from a place of sincere respect and admiration in loving memory of Justice Bentley.

I am a Community Development Worker at the Regent Park Community Health Centre and have been an active participant of the Community Advisory Committee from its inception.

Justice Bentley inspired me from the very first time he spoke with us about restorative justice. He welcomed a multi-sector approach to program development and believed that together we could create a new, progressive and caring strategy by addressing addiction through the provision of a voluntary, court supervised, drug treatment program model with partnership linkages to the community-based service sector.

He was an authentic visionary who opened the space for cooperation and innovative collaboration. Through means of shared resource investment, with a common commitment to the care of individuals who would benefit from the opportunity, we would co-create a viable alternative to the revolving-door incarceration of those whose addiction to illegal street drugs had compromised their health, restricted their life choices and depleted their sense of well-being by repeatedly putting them into conflict with the law.

Initially the experience of speaking with a Judge was so unfamiliar I admit feeling somewhat intimidated, unsure of how to address him. I'd be hesitant, but he would catch my expression and ask me to share my thoughts. Justice Bentley extended his support in such a welcoming and receptive manner that he made it easy for everyone to have a voice at the table.

In fact, he never overlooked a single participant's contribution or made one person feel less important than another, regardless of their profession, position or social status. It's also important to mention that he was an attentive listener and so approachable that he literally tore down any preconceived wall of social division, which is a very difficult thing to do.

Judge Bentley had this quiet strength – a welder of power but practitioner of compassion. A great man of influence yet humble and kind. So humble that he wouldn't even take credit for having been a founder, nor did he see himself as special. But he was.

Having spent numerous hours in various committee meetings sitting alongside Judge Bentley, it is true to say that I observed consistently how well he demonstrated precisely what he expected from everyone involved in all aspects of the Toronto Drug Treatment Program – honesty. I enjoyed his honesty very much.

As clearly witnessed by the amazing legacy of his life's work, he regarded human life as valuable. His collaborative court intervention, drug treatment and holistic community care strategy has worked effectively for more than a decade now, and will continue to thrive in the same supportive spirit of integrity that Justice Bentley modelled and encouraged as the foundational springboard from which our shared vision of hope for positive change in society becomes reality.

Nobody's Neighbours

Why?

If I see, am greeted by and speak with someone many times almost everyday as I go about my neighbourhood, are they not more worthy to be considered and treated as my neighbour than someone who I see only a few times a year as they enter or leave their home? They may live on the same street, yet they have never greeted or spoken a word to me as they pass me in the street – is that person really my neighbour?

Why?

Can I stop in my travels to give one of my neighbours a hug and receive smiles from passers-by but sneers from the very same people when I hug another?

Why?

Is it honourable to donate large sums of money to charitable causes intended to support the very same people that I've been criticized for giving five dollars to?

Why?

Is it acceptable to say, "Oh what a shame," when you see her standing there heavy with child during an extreme heat alert and do nothing but shake your head in disgust at me when I buy her a bottle of water?

To whom it may concern:

Hi, I'm nobody's neighbour so nobody has to care for me.

I'm here awaiting invite yet my name is excluded from your general members list.

Shamed, blamed, avoided and always on the outside looking in.

Stopped at the threshold of every community's door that is opened wide to host complete strangers whom you respectfully treated as welcomed guests.

My contribution is disregard; my wisdom is ignored

I tried to attend your celebrations but I'm shunned and despised

Out of sight out of mind; I can be disposed of with no sense of loss.

Throw away people, in a throwaway society but consider the cost.

My life impact has meaning and I know who I am.

My human imprint is known regardless of reproach and here will I stand.

You may question my very existence but can't see a person of value and dignity

Why?
Btw. - my name is not crackhead.

Sincerely yours,
Nobody's Neighbour

Diana Krecsy

CEO, Calgary Drug Treatment Court Society

For two years I have had the honour of serving as the CEO of the Calgary Drug Treatment Court program. During this time my office door has physically and metaphorically been "open" to ALL drug court participants. Many times I have invited them to come in, and other times they have come in on their own. Posted at the entrance to my office for ALL to see is a poem that has guided my personal belief system and my professional practice as I have had the privilege to work with the participants in our drug court program. It has also served as a daily reminder to me that as human beings, no matter how tough we may look or talk, at our core we are all fragile. We can be wounded and we can break. Sometimes, a single harsh word can pierce like a sword. But not here and not today. In the drug court program and in my office, we are here to be a part of the healing process; of body, mind and soul. We are all in life together.

Diana Krecsy, RN, BN, M.ED. CEO, Calgary Drug Treatment Court Society

Survivors
They are survivors. If you
don't have respect for their
strength you can't be of any
help. It's a privilege that
they let you in - there's no
reason they should trust you
- none. You can't know their
terror - it's your worst
nightmare come true - a
nightmare from which you
never awaken. It's
unrelenting. There has been
no safety; no one, no time,

no place, no thing - All was tainted. Hope was obliterated - time and time again. That they are in your office is in itself a supreme act of valor."

- Author Unknown

Steve S.
Alumni, Toronto Drug Treatment Court

This is a story of Steve Szajko. It's a story that is somewhat the same as others who may have suffered through self-abuse, drug abuse, alcohol abuse. For me it started early. I can remember my first drink at the age of ten, my first smoke, my first pill, my first line, my first hit—you get what I mean. I have tried just about every drug known to mankind, as well as every way to getting high. I think a normal person would probably ask why. Back in the beginning I would have told you to "F off." This attitude, I believe, is because I had something to hide, and I was afraid to tell someone on the account that when I did I was called a liar by family members or told that I was making it up. Does this sound familiar? My abuse really escalated when I turned sixteen. At that point I had already served a year in detention, otherwise known as prison for juveniles, and I had become a survivor of the St. John's Training School. Through this so-called system I had further troubles with more sexual, physical and mental abuse. Again my self-abuse escalated. By the time I was twenty-one I had my first child, and I thank God for him, for now I was faced with a new challenge and this really slowed me down. And then I had my second child. I was blessed with another boy and they were both healthy. For the next fifteen years I became a parent, a caregiver, a provider, and most importantly, a father! And then it happened. I am not pointing fingers, but my partner of seventeen years decided that, for whatever reason, that night I was to be stripped clean of everything I had become and made myself—a coach, a fisher and hunter. I owned my own hunting rifle and was an owner and operator of a business and, most of all, my livelihood – a father. Let's just say I cannot even imagine what she said to the law, but they were not hearing me and they decided that I should not have any contact with my family, nor should I be in Simcoe County, all on the account of my so called "partner"... This was what would fuel my anger that was buried for more than a decade.

This brought the best of the worst of what was to come. I was never violent. I never even had a chance to defend myself, and with this it began. I could not get enough drink and drugs into myself, until my body shut down. I woke up one day, and by this time I came around I was told I nearly died from drugs and alcohol. I was asked to sign a Form 9 or they (the hospital) would do it. That means if they did it, I would have been their property, so I signed and became a patient of what was then called the Addiction Research Foundations (later to become the Center for Addiction and Mental Health). I finished a three-week treatment program and found out a lot about myself that I never would have known. I ended up moving to Toronto and made myself known to most of the local authorities and spent the next thirteen years living a thug's life! I spent more time in local jails than I did on the streets. At one point I was sent a plane ticket from my father and I was on my way out west to British Columbia. Well, instead of things getting better they got really bad. So bad that one evening the Major Crime Unit came and picked me up at my father's residence for questioning. It was about the first murder in BC in January of 2000. After I had been cleared, I was told that I should leave BC right away due to the fact that the RCMP thought it would be in my best interest. So I had to explain to my father how I was not involved. To make a long story short, somebody ripped off a grow-op that belonged to Hells Angels members and it had nothing to do with me other than being in the wrong place at the wrong time. Because my story was checked out by others, I had to show my ID to one of the members and was told not to leave town. Two days had passed; I had never been so scared in my whole life. I would not even take the garbage out. The next day is when the RCMP showed up and then it was on the news and in the local papers – BC's first murder of the year. I read the story and recognized the person that was shot three to five times at point blank in the face. Right then and there, I thought I would take up the advice of my father and the police and was on the next flight back to Toronto. Here I am again, lucky to be here, I thought, and you think that would have scared me straight for the next eight years. I would continue living the lie until something happened to me.

I could not explain it at first. I felt like all the weight of my wrongdoing was on me. The more I thought about it, the harder it seemed to make sense of. Some time ago a seed was planted in me. I was not big on spirituality, but it was clear that I was alone and in jail. The night prior to this, I went to a Bible class where we sang songs and prayed, and it became obvious that the seed that was planted had been watered with the Lord's love that evening, because the next day I felt like all that weight was gone. So I started thinking, and I talked to my lawyer and discussed that I wanted to apply to the Toronto Drug Treatment Court. I had tried it before but used it for a "get-out-of-jail-free card" and I lasted only a month. That was when the program was just new. This time, it would be a different approach. I would do it and be serious about needing the help they were offering this time around. DTC is a hardcore program with lots of demands, but also lots of rewards if and when a person is ready for its challenges. DTC has other supports such as CAMH, John Howard, Women's Own and a few others. I must say, if a person is ready and serious this is one of the best programs around. If you think that you are ready, it's never too late until it's too late, so climb onboard DTC. It helped me, and if I can do it, then anybody can. Thank you to all those involved, especially our belated founder Judge P Bentley.

Poppy Love
Oh dearest Poppy how I envy thee
It is your bittersweet poison that comforts me
When I hug you and take you in my arms
One's too many and a thousand not enough!
Oh my dearest poppy when we were engaged to
be loved I never thought you would totally
drain me more ways than one I can only
imagine how much time, money and other
loved ones I have wasted and hurt please
forgive me my dearest poppy no more aches

Darren M.

Past Participant, Calgary Drug Treatment Court

Michelle L.

Participant, Toronto Drug Treatment Court

DON'T BE FOOLED

DON'T BE FOOLED BY MY SMILING FACE
BECAUSE UNDERNEATH I CRY
I WANT TO SAY I AM HURTING
BUT MY LIFE IS JUST A HIGH

ON THOSE STREETS LIFE IS NO JOKE
WHEN YOU ARE ON THE STREETS TO GET MORE COKE
ALL SPACED OUT AND GETTING COLD
THIS LIFE I LEAD IS MAKING ME OLD

IT`S COLD OUT THERE AND GETTING DAMP
IT`S NOT A HAPPY LIFE LIVING LIKE A CRACKHEAD TRAMP
BUT DON`T BE FOOLED NEXT TIME I SMILE
I AM TRYING TO QUIT BUT IT MIGHT TAKE AWHILE

S. F.
Alumni, Winnipeg Drug Treatment Court

A Road Paved With Good Intentions

Never in my wildest dreams did I ever think that I would ever end up in jail. Who, me? I came from a good middle-class family with no addiction issues, alcoholism or abuse. In my early adulthood I earned a Masters in Educational Psychology in the area of counselling. I was a published author. I was a professional musician. I was a certified teacher and guidance counsellor, hypnotherapist, massage therapist, teacher, English as a second language certified, father, son, friend to many. Yes, I once had had a life. I had promise. I had hope. I had family and friends. Crack robbed me of all of this. By the time I reached Drug Treatment Court, I had lost all my possessions seven times, ended up in treatment seven times, detox seven times, been homeless, broke, picked up cigarette butts on the street, panhandled, the list goes on. I had been to counsellors, rabbis, pastors, physicians, psychologist, psychiatrists, social workers and many other professionals for help. In the end my worst enemy – myself – always led me to trouble, pain, hardship, loss, devastation, dereliction, degradation and despair. Finally, on August 25, 2009, I hit my bottom and did the unthinkable. I had been clean for one year at the time, living in a rural town as a resource teacher and counsellor working with mostly Aboriginal youth. One girl had committed suicide while I was there, and I had the grisly task of cutting her body down from a pole on which she hung. It had a profound effect on me. As counsellor at the school, I had to be there for the students, teachers, administration, parents and community. But who cares for the caretaker? I talked to a counsellor a couple times briefly but really disregarded my own mental health while trying to provide it for others. I believe I suffered some posttraumatic stress from this experience, which was one of the factors leading up to my relapse and offences, as I will now describe.

You see, in Drug Court I learned that I did not do well when I did not have structure in my life, and as a teacher and guidance counsellor I had the summer off, which meant only trouble for me. So, on that unforgettable day in August, I relapsed and truly hit my bottom. I had been using crack all day, had run out of funds, been ripped off, shut out of where I was staying, and felt a sense of hopelessness, loss and futility of my life. I hadn't seen my daughter in over three years, I was divorced, alone, unhappy, unfulfilled, and all I knew was I needed more crack. Not to feel good. Not to feel alive. Not to have a good time or be happy. No, those days of fun in using were long gone. I had no more payday loans available to me. Nothing to pawn or sell anymore, and the thought came into my head that I should rob a fast food restaurant. I walked in not knowing what or how to do this and quickly walked out, deciding not to go ahead with it. And then the synapses in my brain took over. In fact, they demanded more crack. I felt as if I had no choice. Those neurons had to be served. I walked back in and did the unthinkable. I committed my first robbery. Over the next fourteen hours, the fear of getting caught, the fear of going to jail, the thought of the incomprehensible shame, guilt and remorse I may feel later did not even enter my mind. I went from robbery to crack house to the next robbery then back to the pipe over and over and over again until, when I finally was arrested for twelve criminal charges, I honestly felt like saying to the officers, "What took you so long?"

I have been clean and sober since. I spent six weeks in jail and got out on bail and went to a Christian Ministry for a year. My prayers were answered when I finally got accepted into Drug Treatment Court, and from that day my life has just gotten better and better. Not without obstacles or struggles of course. In the year and a half that I was in Drug Court, I never missed an appointment, was on time for every group (except once), never failed a drug screen and always had my eye on the big picture. I will admit that my initial motivation for getting into drug court was to avoid a lengthy jail sentence, but I got so much more than that, and three years later I am still clean and sober, a working, taxpaying, bill-paying, honest, 12-step-working, clean addict. I was very fortunate indeed to meet Michael, the best counsellor I have ever had—and believe me I've had many. He helped me through issues regarding my ex-wife, my daughter, my parents and family, my career, my sense of self and, especially, understanding what self-esteem really is. I feel it has grown immensely since then. He helped me learn that a guy like me needs structure in my life, needs a balanced lifestyle, and that I need to realize what my relapse traps are and how to avoid them. Things like complacency, old habits and lack of self-care – these are all setups for failure to me. Although it was not too challenging for me to stay clean during that time as I had truly hit my ultimate bottom, life issues such as losing my teaching certificates, being separated from my daughter for several years, family dynamics and relationships were things I really needed to wrestle with.

My freedom is so important to me today. I treasure it and will never forget what it was like to lose it. So I put one foot in front of the other. I continue to go for aftercare with my counsellor from Winnipeg Drug Treatment Court. I go regularly to several 12-step meetings. I have a sponsor who I stay in close contact with. I pray and meditate regularly. My relationships with my family are improving. I try to accept the things I am powerless over today and only try and change me.

I always had good intentions. I wanted to please everybody. I wanted to make others proud. Unfortunately my addiction took me to sordid places and robbed me of self-worth. Drug Court taught me that I am not as bad as I thought I was, gave me hope for the future, and literally saved my life. I will always be forever grateful to my counsellor, Michael, and the program of Winnipeg Drug Treatment Court.

Taryn M.
Volunteer, London Drug Treatment Court

I started in January of 2013 as the first-ever London Drug Treatment Court Volunteer. I had previously volunteered with other outreach organizations in London and heard about this program through a friend of mine who thought it would be a good fit with my future goals. Being focused on becoming a police officer, I personally wanted to gain experience with people who are struggling with addiction and mental health. I feel that it's a poorly understood aspect of society, which directly connects to the reality of policing in Canada. I also wanted to develop more of an understanding of the criminal justice system. I felt this would make me understand the reasoning behind criminal behaviour related to addictions. When I took on this role, I had little personal connection to or understanding of addictions and the impact they have on society and individuals. I wanted this to change.

Each week a collaboration of team members meet in court to discuss the progression of the participants in the program. No week will ever be the same, which allows for continual learning. As a outsider who doesn't have much contact with the participants each week, I feel proud of the participants who are doing well in the program and get an opportunity to think about how we can be of assistance to anyone struggling. I sit in court with them each week for them to know I am in full support of their recovery. This is always a powerful experience for me. I'm really pleased with the ways in which volunteering has allowed me to learn about and stand for people suffering from addictions. I just want to take things away from these experiences that I can use in my future career; in this way I hope I can advocate for others in the community.

Being a part of this team has allowed me to see the intensity and power of people's dedication and commitment to making sure these participants have a fighting chance at a second opportunity in life.

All in all, it's giving me insight into these people's lives and struggles, a better understanding of addictions, the ability to begin educating other people in the community, and an understanding of all resources that are available. I see how support and structure can create the presence of accountability and meaning where it didn't exist before. I see how the participants absolutely have the ability to get back on track and create a new life for themselves, and how supporting their recovery can have far-reaching impacts for them personally and for our community and its safety on a much grander scale.

Lindsay D.

Participant, London Drug Treatment Court

The Monster

My addiction, the monster
my ball and chain,
a beast, a demon
a life filled with pain.
As a young teenage girl
I succumbed to addiction
when four men took my youth
with no thoughts of conviction.
Told by authorities
I was to blame
drugged and assaulted
pushed into the game.
I started to hang out
with a pretty bad crowd
and did all sorts of things
that I wasn't allowed.
Escaping reality
day after day
a comfortable numbness
that took me away.
My addiction, the monster
it started to grow
it just kept on feeding
on what I don't know.
I met a nice Harley
that came with a man
a shitload of baggage
and one heavy hand.

I started a job
just shy of eighteen
midnights in a factory
living the dream.
The next several years
went by in a blur
while the monster inside me
continued to stir.
I left my abuser
moved back in with my Mom
I began to despise
the beast I'd become.
Living to use
and using to live
I found myself empty
with nothing to give.
When I realized the monster
had taken control
and was sucking the goodness
right out of my soul.
I knew any moment
the beast would attack
I had to do something
to take my life back.
The number one reason
I stand here today
is you can only hang on
If you give it away.
So good-bye my addiction
we've come to the end
my beast and / or demon
my monster and friend.

Michelle D.
Alumni, Edmonton Drug Treatment Court

LOVE IN THE LIGHT

☆

C.B.
Alumni, Toronto Drug Treatment Court

This is My Story

I was raised in Toronto by both of my parents, a brother and a sister.

I am the youngest; my mom was always working long hours, my dad worked as well.

So my older sister took care of me and my brother. My father was an alcoholic and he was very violent and abusive – my childhood wasn't very pleasant.

I loved sports at a very young age and it was one my favourite hobbies.

I failed grade four because my grades were poor, I was absent from school a lot.

I was also getting into fights; what was going on at home started to bring out a violent side of my personality I didn't know I had.

I started to cause a lot of problems of my own at home. I found some friends who were older; I wanted to fit in so much that I started doing what they were doing, which was committing crimes. It was such an exciting life, having money at a young age and outsmarting cops. I was doing break and enters, shoplifting. It started to become a way of life.

I was in behaviour class from grade six to eight. In grade six I was arrested for my first criminal conviction. I got charged on my thirteenth birthday. I didn't stop there. I was always in trouble with the law, in and out of Juvenile Detention Centers paying for my mistakes. You would think I would have learned my lesson.

I started dating in junior high school only to mess up my relationships because I would cheat on my girlfriends. At fourteen I started hanging around with friends who I thought were cool. We were drinking, smoking and committing crimes, and this is when I was introduced to drugs.

As far as I was concerned, school was done for me and my troubles at home didn't matter to me. I had drugs, women and friends. Who needed family? My friends were my family.

We were a crazy bunch. Our reputation was bad; we created a lot of havoc in our community.

I was using drugs and drinking and committing crimes every day; I liked the carefree life and didn't want to stop. At sixteen my mom gave me a choice: either I went to school or I worked. She said she would put me out of the house if I didn't change my life, she got me a job working with her and it lasted for a few years. I was using drugs and alcohol even on my workdays. I couldn't handle it anymore. I knew I could make money by selling drugs; everyone I knew was doing it and I wanted a piece of the "PIE".

I started to live with one of my ex-girlfriends for over a year and was making a lot of money. I started to live the high life— going out to restaurants, strip clubs and taking taxis everywhere. 'Life was good' until I started to get curious about the drugs I was selling.

I started using my own product, in a few days I was hooked. I couldn't stop.

So I started stealing to pay back my drug dealers. I burned every bridge I had and was in and out of jail often. This continued for over 10 years.

I almost died a few times. My addiction was killing me; jail was the safest place for me to be. I would get my rest just to get out and do the same thing over and over again.

It wasn't until August 2011, when I gave the Drug Treatment Court another try.

I had tried years ago, but like everything else in my life I had tried, I had failed.

Immediately upon entering the program, I went on a run and began using again. I was helpless.

I couldn't ask for help while I was using. I got picked up on more charges and Toronto Drug Treatment Court gave me another chance. I got out and used again, but my using wasn't as frequent. I was using a few days a week, which was a great improvement. I started believing in myself that eventually I could do this, so I followed the guidelines that the program had to offer. I was getting help from the entire therapist team in the program and I was doing the work – not using, showing up for court and to all of my groups.

It was an amazing feeling, I was on my way.

Trish G.
Participant, London Drug Treatment Court

Lost Girl
You can look at my face
because my pain doesn't show
I'd have to tell you, how the
hurt grows and grows
Every day I struggle trying
to make up for lost time
but I've been there, I've done that
I fought a battle, I lost my mind.
Twisted and torn
my heart full of scars
my arms full of tracks
from shading for the stars.
I could never get high enough
to take my pain away
I cry when I'm sleeping, so no one
sees me that way.
Take a good look
do you like what you see?
Trust me I'm ugly, you don't want
to know me
Something you love, once yours
is now mine
even most men are just
dollar signs
so the next time "they" say
here's a hit
it's for you
go slow and with caution
or this girl could be you.

Untitled

Baby I'm sorry I missed a whole
year of your life
Mommy did some things that
weren't very nice
I know at this moment
you can't understand, but I know
that in time,
answers you'll demand.
Yes, I do love you
I love you so much
and yes baby girl, you were
more than enough
I'm sorry you're judged and
have a chip on your shoulder
I pray every day it gets smaller
as you grow older.
I let certain things consume me
till I was broken down
but mommy found it so hard
to sleep not having you around
And it breaks my heart to
say that cause you'll never
be my excuse
it's just without you
there is no me, you're my
walking, talking proof.
You're everything that's real to me
You're everything that counts
You're my heart, my soul
my blood, my tears
in bucket full amounts.

Robin Cuff

Manager, Toronto Drug Treatment Court

In 1999, being one of the community service providers summoned by Justice Paul Bentley to support this new venture called Drug Treatment Court, I was thrilled to know that someone had the passion and the drive to do something – anything – for the people we saw caught up in this unforgiving cycle. At that time, I was pleased to be part of the partnership but never, ever considered that one day I would be a part of the Toronto Drug Treatment Court team. Eleven years later, I found myself leading the treatment team at the Centre for Addiction and Mental Health.

I have spent nearly fifteen years in the addictions field, and my life has been made tremendously richer with each position I have held and each client I have served. I believe that if we are humble enough to realize we are not the experts, our clients are, there is so much we can learn about addiction, mental health, courage, trauma, healing, pain, resilience, recovery and the many other parts of the complex lives our clients have lived and continue to live. I have learned much. I have been so privileged and blessed to work in this field and to work in this program. I have been privileged to work with people whose values are so solidly rooted in caring for others, generating hope and offering choice. I have been given the gift of trust many times over by people who have absolutely no reason to trust anyone connected to this system and that is something I will always treasure.

As I write this, I struggle with what to say. On the one hand, there is so much that can be said to portray my passion and love for what I do, and on the other hand, it is difficult to know what words to use to make a positive impact on anyone who might read these words.

I have decided to focus on the process and I hope I can communicate through these inadequate words that recovery is not a straight line. It is not found through a formula and certainly is not "one size fits all." It is not as simple as just stopping use, and just stopping use does not always simply stop the activities surrounding the use. It is a process, which is often frustrating and painful and which zig zags, often to the point of chaos and crisis. It is about the whole person. It is about relationships. It is about hope.

"Locked up" flows off their tongues at times
As if a state, merely benign
Betrays frustration, anger, fear
Layered pain, but not a tear

"Locked up" and forced to live inside
Watched, controlled, nowhere to hide
In and out – the revolving door
Crimes and charges, the familiar lore

"Locked up" the burden of their souls
What else to do but play the roles?
Rough and tough without a care
No victim here, just boosting wares

"Locked up" with labels firmly placed
Designed for guilt, shame, and disgrace.
Their spirits shred, their hope is gone
Too many times been trampled on.

"Locked up" the person fades away
And people hold their love at bay
The search for happiness pursues
But what they find is just a ruse.

"Locked up" the world is oh so small
Attempts to change just hit a wall
Crack and smack and crystal meth
As dear to them as their next breath

"Locked up" a vicious pleasure quest
A chaos, pain and danger fest
And yet inside a yearning still
To dare escape the crushing mill

"Locked up" and left unspoken, dreams
Afraid of hope without the means
To resurrect the feelings numbed
And wonder what I could become

"Locked up" is more than just a cell
A symbol of a hope dispelled
For freedom seems a far-fetched dream
A life so lost can be redeemed?

"Freedom" comes but never stays
Released from jail back to the fray
To change their lot, a worthy goal
But how to heal a wounded soul?

"Freedom" cannot be bought or sold
Elusive at times and hard to hold
"Do I deserve this?" I'm not sure
Present and future, all a blur

"Freedom" offered, but there are terms
Continued freedom must be earned
Attend the groups, the screens and court
And if you use you must report

"Freedom" but do I get to choose
Follow the rules or else I lose?
Try it out, but still not clear
Can I make it through a year?

"**Freedom**" hard to grasp it still
Change is tough and all uphill
But little by little one day at a time
A life restored can be mine

"**Freedom**" from jail is just one step
Addiction throws a wider net
The grief and loss are very real
Do I risk it? Can I feel?

"**Freedom**" gives another chance
To change my ways and change my stance
Forgotten worth to be revived
Brand new reasons for which to strive

"**Healing**" a journey just begun
Not thinking of when I'll be done
Building foundations strong to last
Cannot build upon my past

"**Healing**" I get to choose it now
To never break another vow
And yet I know my weakness still
The drug, the crime, the search for thrill

"**Healing**" is slow, there's sometimes pain
And often hard to see the gain
But now I see that pleasure fades
And thrills and highs aren't meant to stay

"**Healing**" allows a light to shine
Clear thoughts are flowing through my mind
So hard for me to give my trust
Rely on others now I must

"Healing" my spirit, body, mind
Grieving what I leave behind
It helped but, in a flash, was gone
It used me up, I was its pawn

"Healing" laughter, feeling real
Revealing things I had concealed
Puzzle pieces fitting in
Not a game to lose or win

"Healing" has indeed begun
Lifetime journey never done
Fear of failure and success
All that's asked – to give my best

"Hope and choice" are mine to claim
Once "locked up," now "freedom" gained
Free to tell my secret dreams
Free to choose the ways and means

"Hope" that even I can own
On the journey, not alone
The things I want, now I can see
Possible, for even me

And **"Choice"** was taken from my hands
Now given back, I understand
I get to choose my path each day
With help, I choose a better way

I was **locked up** but **freedom** now
Healing begun, I now know how
With **hope** my future can be bright
My daily **choice** to fight this fight.

-Robin Cuff, 2013

☆

Wendy H.
Participant, Calgary Drug Treatment Court

CLEAN `N` SOBER

I can now look in the mirror
And say to my self,
Wow you look good, when you are,
Clean `n` Sober.

I have walked a lot of streets,
In the City of Calgary
I met a lot of people
Who have said, you look good
Clean `n` Sober

I walk my path
Each and every day,
I can now finally say,
I AM "365" days
Clean `n` Sober

This Is My Story

I am going to tell a story
So many of us know
It's hard to do one
And then to say no

I grew up when it was always around me
My mom and dad always did it
The one they could not do was to admit it.

I lost my mother, and didn't know my father
I was raised by my grandmother and grandfather

My mother was 32, when I went to her funeral
I was only 8 when I should have said
Mom I DO LOVE YOU!!

I met my father once when I was too young
If I another chance, it would be a happy one.

This is my story I share with you
I may not know you, but I pray for you.

One more thing, God Bless you too,

K. M.
Participant, Winnipeg Drug Treatment Court

My Story

To say I have lived an interesting life would be an understatement. Growing up as a policeman's daughter with my mother also working for the police department, you would never have expected me to end up going through some of the things that I have. But thanks to drug and alcohol addiction I ended up doing things I never thought I would ever do.

I grew up in a nice suburb in Winnipeg Manitoba, with a pool in the backyard, and I was always taken care of by my loving parents. I was able to be involved in sports at the young age of four. I played all kinds of sports, such as ringette, soccer, basketball and volleyball, and I was also a competitive diver at a young age. I basically had everything a kid could dream of. As a kid, I remember the only time I felt good was when I was playing sports. I never really had a lot of friends and got picked on and made fun of all the time by the kids in school. There were a number of days out of the month that I would end up coming home crying because of other kids, but when I played sports I felt alive, because I was actually good at something and the girls on my teams actually liked me. I remember in grade seven, I started making friends in school and they were in the "popular" crowd. I was very happy about this and was actually getting some confidence in myself because I had friends. The very first time I was invited to a party I was ecstatic. I didn't know what to expect, but just the fact I was included was good enough for me. That very first party was the first time I ever consumed alcohol in my life. I was thirteen years old, all I wanted to do was fit in and thought it was harmless because everyone else was doing it and there was no way I was going to say no and look like a loser in front of everyone. At thirteen years old you don't think about the future or what drinking can do; I never would have guessed that I would end up as an IV crystal meth user and in jail.

From the moment I tried alcohol, I was hooked. That feeling of confidence I got was like nothing I had ever felt before. I continued to drink every weekend pretty much throughout the rest of junior high. Once I entered high school, I ended up making it onto the women's hockey team, where I was able to have a bunch of friends and I felt a part of a group, but my life still revolved around partying on the weekends. I started using marijuana, which I would smoke on a daily basis. I did really well in school and in hockey even though that was not my focus; when it came time to graduate and think about university I just did what my parents wanted me to do, which was get into university and pursue a career.

I had other plans, of course. I was heavily into cocaine and other drugs by this point and was selling weed because I thought it was cool. I was really good at living a double life, making sure I looked good in my family's eyes while doing things that they had no idea about. Naturally, I ended up dropping out of school close to the same time that I started getting in trouble with the law. I always thought I was untouchable to getting in trouble or getting hooked on drugs, maybe because I grew up pretty sheltered to what really can go on in the world. Also, because of my dad being a cop, I really thought I could never get in trouble and that no matter what I did my dad could fix it and it would go away. That, of course, was not the case, as I ended up getting hooked onto crystal meth and in a matter of six months I had lost my job, car, family and home. I also lost about thirty pounds and looked like I was thirty-five at the age of twenty-two. When I ended up in jail, I remember thinking I would get out right away because I was the daughter of a cop who had never been in real trouble before, but when they didn't let me out, I was devastated. Here I was, an eighty-pound girl from a nice family, in the Winnipeg Remand Centre with no idea when I would get out.

I tried to make the best of it, but it was not easy. I ended up going to a treatment center for about eleven months. It was a place that took people in jail and tried to teach you different behaviours so you wouldn't use or do crime. That didn't work for me, because the day I left I was back at it and it wasn't long before I ended up back in the Remand Center. This time, though, I was told about a program called Drug Court because the Crown had mentioned it to my lawyer. I was willing to try anything, so I met with Wayne and they accepted me into the program.

It was hard for me at first to stay sober and realize I really had a problem, but the people at Drug Court believed in me when I didn't believe in myself. And the best part is that instead of putting me back in jail and throwing away the key, they gave me a chance to go back to rehab and get integrated into AA in the city and really find my footing to become a productive member of society, and I will be forever grateful to them for that. I look at my life today and really have to thank Drug Court, because I would not have the things I do today if that program hadn't been there for me.

I am actively in AA and sponsoring other women. I actually have my own apartment and I pay bills with my own money that I work for. I also recently signed up for university again and will be starting in January. In my eyes, Drug Court gives people like me a second chance to change their lives and to realize that we deserve a good life, no matter what we have done in the past. All I can really say is that if I didn't have the privilege to be in Drug Court, I would either still be incarcerated or would not be alive today.

E.C.
Alumni, Toronto Drug Treatment Court

For every moment in life where I thought I just couldn't, I've now discovered that I can. My name is E.C. I became a client of the Toronto
Drug Treatment Court on November 17th, 2011, and have been clean
and sober from Crystal Methamphetamine since January 11th, 2012. I
am thirty-two years old today and stand proud of finally being able to
exercise the power of choice, leaving behind what seems to be thirty-
one years of constant invalidation of my human existence; experiences
of sexual, emotional and physical abuse coupled with memories of loss,
which have devastated me for many years. Choice never seemed to be
an option for me once the nightmare of using took over; I was a slave
and a victim of my past. Drugs clouded my mind. Drugs put on hold a
much-needed healing period and rendered me unable to remember all
the good and success I've had in my lifetime, as well. Drug Treatment
Court has helped me transition these memories of abuse into exactly
that; today my past heartaches are nothing but a memory and my success
lives on. My future has yet to be defined, but today, more importantly, I
choose to be a human being who isn't "just existing" in this world. I am
participating to the best of my ability in life with each day getting easier
and easier. I expect days that are more difficult than others, but each day
I am sober is another day where I've participated in life, and that to me
is a big accomplishment.

Today, I can choose to see life through the filter of choice, and I try
everyday not to define myself by my mistakes or by my past negative
experiences. I am slowly replacing the filter of a victimized boy with a
grown man who is capable of choosing for himself. What helps me to be
successful is granting myself the gift of a very difficult but very necessary
emotional transition of being able to forgive myself. The very essence of
humanity is that we are imperfect beings. Only by making mistakes can
we learn, only by making mistakes can we discover and only by making
mistakes can we become humble. I do my best everyday, and so long as

my best is what I do then my mistakes can now be learning opportunities for a better future.

Drug Treatment Court is filled with people who care, who listen and who come to work everyday smiling. It has become clear that passion for their work is the one guiding emotion relevant to each staff member of the DTC. Every member in DTC – Judges, Lawyers, Crown Attorneys, Therapists, Doctors, Peer Support Workers, Clients and many others – has been a vehicle of inspiration to my new discovery that today I CAN do this; today I CAN choose to do this and today I CAN have faith that I will do this...I am finally not ALONE.

To other members of DTC across Canada, new members, existing members or our dear alumni members, I leave you with this to remember: Even when it feels like you can't, time will show you that "you CAN!" Never give up! DTC and its members clearly have shown me faith and they believed in me. They have allowed me to dream once again. So long as there is faith in your mind and belief in yourself, so long as you NEVER give up, DTC will not give up on you.

Joanne Short

Former Therapist, Toronto Drug Treatment Court

Graduation Speech for my Client, Wayne

The only difference between "try" and "triumph" is a little "ump".

Good afternoon, Judge Bentley, members of the Drug Treatment Court court team, members of the Drug Treatment Court treatment team, clients of the Drug Treatment Court program, your friends and families.

Firstly, I just want to say how thrilled I was to be asked to come here today and say a few words on behalf of one of your graduates. I'm so happy to be a part of celebrating a certain young man's journey into unknown territory that began two years ago in this courthouse, in the Honourable Judge Bentley's Drug Treatment Court. It really felt heart-warming to be able to bear witness to the hardships this client battled, the obstacles he encountered along the path of recovery, and the strength and commitment with which he maintained his courage in the face of both. Today marks the day when he can say he achieved the goals he originally set out to achieve and that he can let go of the past and head full force into the future. I truly celebrate this day and feel privileged to be a part of this poignant moment in time, both *for* you and *with* you.

It was a cold wintery day in February 2009, when Wayne, encouraged by legal counsel, made a final decision to join the DTC program. He had just obtained some reasonable housing outside of the shelter system at that time and wanted to keep it. So, if he could work on his court issues through this program, he thought that maybe he could sustain a more stable way of life.

When he arrived at the Centre for Addiction and Mental Health on that cold day in February, I was struck by his resemblance to the famous actor of a similar name, John Wayne. He had sort of a slow, meandering kind of gait, a mellow, distinctive, and softly spoken voice – when he did speak, that is – and a kind of imposing height, with a slight bend at the neck that made me think he might burst into some soothing cowboy ballad at any moment.

When I think of Wayne, I think of a quiet, unassuming, and perhaps clumsily gentle kind of man who, when he joined the DTC program, one might have detected an ever-so-mild bit of resistance. Despite his stated commitments, there were times when he challenged me with the task of making sure things were fair and equitable for everyone. In his own words, Wayne reflected in a recent conversation we had, "I fought it at first."

At the same time, Wayne demonstrated a moral fibre, which guided his life on many levels and kept him within the boundaries of the values he holds dear to his heart – values of honesty and integrity, and respect for others, rules, ethical procedures, and for himself.

When I think of Wayne, I think of a man always helping somebody – a man who has genuine concern and personal regard for the world and the people in it, easily exemplified through his volunteer work at a local church where he works closely with the pastor, making sure people get enough food, repairing things around the church, and walking the pastor's dog for him. It was often that we'd see him rounding a corner onto the "3 west" hallway at [the Centre for Addiction and Mental Health location at] Russell Street, with a sort of friendly curl to his mouth, a nod of his head, and a tip of his hat, and I was sure I could hear him saying in the notable, John Wayne kind of way, "Yaws ma'm, I'm here to help, yaaas ma'm".

But I would be remiss if I failed to make note of the man we watched developing as W. W. made changes to his substance use life. As a chrysalis unfolds, Wayne started showing us his many skills and the confidence he had to put them into action. From a man who would say at the beginning of practically every session with me for at least the first year, "I don't say much, ya know, I don't talk very much – I don't like to share things or talk about myself, especially in a group, and I haven't got much to say, ya know," to a man who became one of the friendliest clients on "3 west" – engaging vocally in the spirit of the program, promoting its benefits, and defending its value. He gradually but visibly began to change his mantra to sound more like, "I don't know what it is about you people, but somehow you get me to talk." A lot, in fact. Often during a session with me, he would get up as if to leave, conveying that he was finished talking, or so I thought – and the next thing I knew he would be back in the chair, still talking – and apparently nowhere near finished. Change was in the air, and Wayne's journey epitomized the change process, not only by this example alone, but by all the work he did – the work that brought him to this day, in this courthouse – in the courtroom where he began his work two years ago.

It wasn't anything in the program that "got" Wayne to talk. It wasn't anything I did. It wasn't any magic in the air. It was Wayne – listening and working the program, using what it offered him, those were the things that resulted in the changes he made. It was him – Wayne, "chairman of the board" Wayne, "Wayne Ltd." – that grabbed life back and took control of his world.

There is an archway in Johannesburg, South Africa, put there during the economic crisis of some years ago, that has etched in it the words "without change there would be no butterflies". Without our clients, there would be no change. And with their changes, they go confidently in the direction of their dreams to live the lives they were meant to live.

Reclaiming the person he was meant to be, Wayne represents, for Drug Treatment Court, what Drug Treatment Court can do to inspire people to change.

Thank you for that legacy, Wayne. You put the "umph" in "triumph".

When we were asked to stand today as court convened, we were asked to do so with the words "all rise". I believe I speak for everyone, Wayne, when I say to you: today, we all rise.

Congratulations.

Shanon B. F. F.

Participant, London Drug Treatment Court

My name is Shanon Burton Ferguson-Feit.

I was born in Richmond Hill, Ontario, and was raised in the rougher part of Toronto until the age of seven. Then my family and I lived in Truro, Nova Scotia, until I was fifteen. While there I got involved in smoking pot and breaking the law, and I rebelled against the world. At fifteen, my family and I moved back to Ontario, London this time, and I started getting involved in even more drugs, and with that came the crime lifestyle. I was in and out of jail for eight years. During those eight years, I spent five-and-a-half behind bars. During those five years I got involved in a lot more drugs – ecstasy, pot, mushrooms, crack, acid, and benzos. The last drug I got involved in was morphine, and that put me right under. I got quickly and badly addicted; my life went downhill pretty fast. I lost everything – my job, the respect of my family, my self-respect, my house, and my health. I went to jail in the summer of 2010 for a break and enter trying to support my habit. I got into Drug Treatment Court in London and I was involved in that for fourteen months. During the first bit of that time, I was a wreck—mentally, physically, and emotionally. Drug Treatment Court helped me through it all, especially my counsellor and judge. Then I had a bad day and ended up back in jail on an eighteen-month sentence. In July 2012, I was granted parole, by the grace of God, and was released to a treatment center. I am continuing my treatment and when I leave this place I am going to better my life and myself.

I hope that one day someone can read my poem and relate to what I have written.

Thank You

There was a time I needed someone in my corner
You guys showed up, Addiction Services Drug Court, Jim, John Howard
and His Honour

All through the ups and especially the down
You were there for me, you turn my life around.
You pulled my body from its drug-induced host.
I was torn apart inside, from coast to coast
I didn't realize just what I had; I took it all for granted my way of life
was bad.
Through injection morphine was the choice.
Now I am off it, through you I rejoice.
But don't get down, because of where I am
Just remember, God holds my plan
So don't think you failed because of you I now see a light

You did a lot for me; I now know how to live right
Stop all the lies, and face life's facts.
Slow down a bit, learn how to relax.
Put one foot in front of the other, baby steps if need be.
Take it small and slow, just steadily.
Live my life only on life's terms.
When you learn that, everything turns.
I now know my life and what I need to do.
All of this thanks to all of you.
I wasn't arrested I was rescued.

Oh yeah, did I mention this was all thanks to all of you

Yours truly,
Shanon Feit

Thank you

There was a time I needed, someone in my corner.
You guys showed up, addiction services, drug court, Jim, John
Howard and his Honor.
All through the ups, and especially the downs.
You were there for me, you turned my life around
You pulled my body, from it's drug induced host.
I was torn apart inside, from coast to coast.
I didn't realize, just what I had.
I took it all for granted, my way of life was bad.
Through injection, morphine was the choice.
Now I'm off it, through you'd rejoyce.
But don't get down, because of where I am.
Just remember, God holds my plan.
So don't think you failed because of you'd now see a
light.
You've did alot for me, I now know how to live right.
Stop all the lies, and face lifes facts.
Slow down a bit, learn to relax.
Put one foot in front of the other, baby steps if
need be.
Take it small and slow just steadily.
Live my life only on lifes terms.
When you learn that everything turns.
I now know my life, and what I need to do.
All of this, thanks to all of you.
I wasn't arrested, I was rescued.
Oh yeah did I mention this was all thanks to
all of you

Yours
Truely
Shawn B

Donald J. E.

Participant, London Drug Treatment Court

Hello, my name is DJ. This is my story.

I was born on April 30, 1981, in London, Ontario. While growing up, I encountered many troubles during my childhood. Every year was a new school and a new problem.

The real problem was always being the new kid, so I was the first to be bullied and it was hard for me, especially the fact of never having my dad there for me. My dad left my mom when I was two years old, because he was a married man and went back to his family.

About six years later, in 1988, my mom tried to move on when my brother Nate was born. I never got along with anybody that got with my mom, because I thought I was the man of the house. Nate's dad didn't stick around and like my father, he left. I hated seeing my mom so upset all the time.

In 1993, my mom met her current husband, and a year later my youngest brother, Robert, was born. Robert's dad and I did not get along at all. That's when I started drinking and smoking pot. I was twelve years old and alcohol made me feel like there were no rules to life at all. I started hanging with the bad kids and getting in trouble.

By the time I was sixteen, I already had my first criminal charges. That's when I was introduced to cocaine and it made me feel invincible. Cocaine took away my so-called problems. I was skipping school, fighting, and breaking the law. I eventually dropped out of school, joined a gang, got arrested, and was sent to Bluewater Youth Facility (secure youth custody). I met more contacts in the criminal lifestyle. When I was twenty, I joined another gang, and for the next four years it was jail time after jail time.

When I was twenty-four, I met the mother of my daughters, moved to Toronto, and started working at a restaurant. My first daughter was born on Jan 5th, 2006. I was so happy to be a father for the first time. I was doing so well in Toronto; I was only drinking a little. When we moved back to London to be with family, we had our second daughter. She was born on April 17, 2008.

I put my kids and their mother through hell during my addiction. I was a good father but was hooked on oxys. In late 2010 we split up and I was really hitting rock bottom. That's when my friend Jamison reached out to me and told me about another way of life – the "recovery way". This is when I first met my current sponsor, Kevin, a.k.a. "Muffin". I lived with them until I got into a recovery home, but three months into living in the recovery home I started to go downhill.

I relapsed badly. This went on for a year, and during that time I met my girlfriend, Natasha. I put her through hell, but she still backed me up and put up with my crap. In January 2012, we found out she was pregnant. A couple weeks later I was in jail for charges that I had picked up during my relapse. I spent four months in there, and just before I got out my sponsor, Kevin, came to visit me and I told him I was ready to surrender to recovery once again.

When I was released from jail I entered the London Drug Treatment Court. My lawyer was the one that got me in this, and for that I'd be forever grateful. Since my release on April 17, 2012, which is also my youngest daughter's birthday, I have been clean and sober. My son was born on September 16, 2012, and my life is amazing right now thanks to my sponsor, my family, my friends, my girlfriend, and my kids. I also want to give a special thanks to my lawyer, L.D.T.C., and Addiction Services for giving me the chance to shine again. "God bless."

William A.

Alumni, Vancouver Drug Treatment Court

My Name Is Bill

My name is Bill and I am a grateful recovery addict.

I have been in my addiction for thirty-five years. Along with my addiction came criminal activities.

The consequences were jail. I had reached a lifetime flow and I prayed to God to help me, a few days later I heard about the Drug Treatment Program

I was interested and ready for a change in my life.

I was accepted in the Drug Treatment Program and my life changed 180 degrees.

I was assigned to a recovery home.

The Drug Treatment Program does work; I graduated and have a whole new outlook on life and I am living a much better life.

Thanks to Drug Court.

Thank you.

Pamela Spurvey

Peer Support Worker, Edmonton Drug Treatment Court

My Story As Told To A Local Newspaper
And A Community Newsletter

"I remember being on my knees in a jail cell and signing my kids over to the care of someone else. I felt broken. But I had so many reasons to get better, and when I decided to get better, that was the best choice I could have ever made."

Pamela was homeless, addicted to crack cocaine and crystal meth in Camrose, Alberta. She grew up as the daughter of a drug-addicted prostitute and eventually began dealing crack cocaine and crystal meth herself.

Her five children were taken away and she was arrested and charged with several counts of drug trafficking. Pamela ended up in the Edmonton Drug Treatment and Community Restoration Court. She's still there now – as an addictions peer support worker.

Through her time in the Drug Treatment Court, her kids were her main motivation. "Seeing the change in my children has kept me strong," she says. "My kids always tell me they're proud of me and that they love having their mom back. That's the part that keeps me clean."

"The help's not going to come to you, and you have to want it. Recovery is something you're going to have to do for the rest of your life. This is a disease. I have to continue and struggle everyday, and it's not going to go away."

As a peer support worker, she aims to give back to others who are struggling with addiction. "When I'm helping people, I want to save them, but the best I can do is share my story and give them a piece of me, to use my choices as an example for what can happen, what you can do if you choose to."

My daughters have written letters for me, which I would like to share:

My Mother
by CS, age 14

Mom, you do so much for everyone and never expect anything in return. You are the strongest woman I know. Our family has been through so much, but no matter what, we never let ourselves fall apart. I know I put you through so much, and never once did you forget to tell me you loved me, even though I was lost for a really long time. You are the only person I know who is as courageous as you are. You worked your butt off to be where you are today, and even when times get rough you always make everything right again. Just know everything you do is appreciated by us. It may seem like we take the things you do for us for granted, but we do not. You taught me more things about life than you could imagine. I may not show it, but Mom, if it were not for you, I would not be where I am today. The last three years of school, I did not see myself graduating; I took many wrong paths but you always made sure you put me on the path I was meant to be on. Even though I still make mistakes, you are still there to always wrap your arms around me and tell me it will be okay. Together we have been through hurricanes and sunshine days, but at the end of it all we never forget to say I love you. You are the most beautiful women I know, and of course, look at me; I had to get my looks from someone. I never gave up on knowing you would make it in sobriety, because look at you. I know my mother is strong-willed, and she has the most courage and has a big heart filled with love. You are the one who taught me how to believe in myself and how to never give up on something that means a lot to me. You are my role model, Mom, and I could not think of anyone better. I look up to you, and I know I am getting older now and I will make more mistakes, but knowing I have such a great mom to lean on makes it all so much better. My life is amazing because of you. Even through our hardest times, I knew in my heart we would pull through together. I love you so much, no words can explain it. In case I do not tell you this enough, I am so proud of you and I am so proud of how much you have grown. You are not only my best friend, you are the world's greatest mother. No matter what words are said between us or what fights we get in, I love you. This is everything

I feel and everything I think that will never change. I love you so much, Mommy. Thanks for giving me another great Christmas!

XOXOXO; CS

My Mommy
by "The BOSS," age 12

First of all, I want to wish you a very merry Christmas! You put so much hard work into raising us and trying to make our lives happy every moment. I want you to know I appreciate every single thing you do for me, even if it is as little as buying me my favourite foods. I appreciate it all. You put your all into everything you do for us. It makes me so happy to see you do things for yourself once in awhile, you definitely deserve it. You may get stressed out sometimes, but know I love you and I am here for you (unless you're stressed 'cause of me, L.O.L.) I will try to do my best to help you out. I am so fortunate to have a family like I do and to have a mother like you to grow up with and remember one day. I love that even though life can be very hard for you, you stay strong until you get through it. Moms, there are so many moments when I wish you knew how much you matter to me and how much I thank you for being such a wonderful mother. If there is happiness in my heart, it is because you help put it there. If there is gentleness in my beliefs, it is because you showed me how to care. If there is understanding in my thinking, it is because you shared your wisdom. If there is a rainbow over my shoulder, it is because of your outlook and vision. If there is a knowledge that I can reach out and really can make dreams come true, it is because I learned from the best teacher of all—I learned from you. In the times of my life whether we are near of far, please remember, Mom, you will always be my best friend and there could never be any mother more wonderful than my own precious mother. I love you so much, Mommy, and I hope you have an awesome Christmas!

With all the love I have to give,

The BOSS

Mahad E.

Alumni, Toronto Drug Treatment Court

I will try to describe in these following few paragraphs to the best of my recollection how it was, what happened, and how it is now in regards to my drugs and alcohol addiction among many others addictions. During the height of my addiction, I always thought that I would stay a recidivist petty criminal who would spend most of his time inside correctional institutions more than the shelters, streets, and underneath the bridges that I used to called residences.

I came to Canada when I was ten years old, about a quarter-century ago, with my family. I don't really know if the fact that I grew up with my step-mom, that I haven't seen my biological mom since I left my native country, and that I haven't really had a father figure to look up to contributed to my addiction. Needless to say that I never felt good in my own skin, and when I started smoking marijuana, four years later, I had found something that made me forget the world for a brief moment. Ever since then, I have been chasing that elusive feeling. My drug addiction escalated and led me to make bad decisions. It started directing my feelings and thoughts. When I first experimented with crack cocaine, I thought that I'd finally arrived to the Promised Land, because it helped render me oblivious to everything that was happening around me, and at the same time numbed those dreaded feelings of guilt and shame. The obsession of that next hit on the pipe would ultimately lead me to my demise. I knew that I had a huge problem and tried on my own to quit but couldn't muster to put a few weeks together. I've tried a lot of different methods to tackle these overwhelming habits that I've developed for the past twenty-odd years. I relocated to another city, got married, had kids, changed friends and jobs but was unable to quit the drugs. At the end, I became unemployable, untrustworthy, distant, homeless, and cared about nothing but getting high. I honestly thought that I would spend the rest of my life as an addict who would amount to nothing.

That was until I came across the Drug Treatment Program during one of my regular visits to the bullpen at Old City Hall. This program, that was founded by the late Justice Bentley, god bless his soul, and administered in conjunction with the good people of CAMH, has truly saved my life.

I will never forget what this program has done for me. It has given me back my life and from the beginning treated me as a human being with dignity and respect. It believed in me and never gave up on me, even when I did. Today, I have my kids and family back in my life. I have a full-time job and a boss who thinks that I'm a responsible, reliable employee and who's even willing to invest in my future by paying my tuition. I would never been able to stay sober without the help of Tanya, Paulette, Justice Bentley, Annie, Justice Hogan, Justice Omatsu, Dave, Josie, and even the prosecutor, Mr. Wilson. There are many others that are eluding me right now, and if I've left you out, I sincerely apologize. I will always be grateful to you all.

Merci Beaucoup,
M.E.

Jeffery C.
Alumni, Edmonton Drug Treatment Court

Through perseverance, hard work, and dedication, I have endured through eighteen years of active addiction and the despair that accompanied such a life. With twelve years of incarceration and another seven before me, I was accepted into Edmonton's Drug Treatment Community Restoration Court. What may have been my last chance to get out from under, I gave it my all, graduating with honours in July 2011. Shortly after, Vancouver's Drug Court Judge, Jocelyn Palmer, united my beautiful wife and I on Palm Beach, B.C., and today I am a happy man. With new life, new meaning, I have embarked on a helping journey with Y.M.C.A. and an education in social work. It is my aim to help those still suffering, to be there to walk others out from under. There is hope, and we must embrace it.

Off on past

Lost in time, a moments still
Looking on to futures will
Seeing smiles, wondering why
Wishing the world was kind to I

With hope fast fading
The sun's dark shading
I cried out......help, help
Heard I was, the kindness felt

As times did change
New dreams within range
Life changing, taking its turn
Was what I deserved

Upon this world as I walk
Views, morals and values caught
Into the real, the here and now
Leading on, now knowing how

No more harm, none be done
Help to those still in the run
I am not lost, as I once was
Here I am, as a good man does

Under the arbor, in the sun
Meaning found, love has won
Into the future, from hard times past
Happy in life, hope at last

Derrick S.
Participant, London Drug Treatment Court

Change is Possible

People clearly can change, if the people around us believe us that change is possible. Finding myself as a participant in the London Drug Treatment Court Program was an opportunity for me to identify and overcome challenges and obstacles that lead to substance abuse and crime. I've spent a very large part of my life in and out of prison for property-related crimes, and addiction had become an overwhelming destructive force that encompassed my thinking and my ability to believe in myself. I remember sitting in the local detention centre feeling worthless and helpless, wanting to give up on myself. But giving up on myself has never been an option that rested well within.

Having heard about the Drug Treatment Court Program, I decided to look into it through my lawyer. At first, things were very much up in the air as to whether or not I qualified, but through the grace of god and the powers to be, I was admitted in the Drug Treatment Court Program and given a certificate congratulating me on my acceptance into the Program. I remember thinking to myself that this program was going to be everything that I ever needed to help me to become that person that I wanted to be and not that person that I had become.

My best interpretation of the Drug Treatment Court Program would be to describe it as a collaboration of community resources that provides an addict with an individualized plan to deal with issues of addiction that lead to crime. The program provides an integrated approach to addiction and criminal issues, as well as behaviour issues. This integration of community resources has expectations of each participant, and in the beginning I was kept quite busy with attendance at various appointments and groups.

I remember thinking to myself that this program was going to be everything that I needed it to be if I was ever going to become that person that I wanted to be.

During the period of time that I was involved with the Drug Treatment Court Program, I was fortunate to have been able to have an opportunity to develop a support network of not only the participants, but other people, such as addiction services. The John Howard Society, St. Leonard's Society, and many other community resources as well— members of these groups formed a team, and every single member of this team was not only supportive but was caring as well. Each and every one of these people not only invested time into me, but they also invested a part of themselves into me when it came to helping me to believe in myself and to not beat myself up as I had been so accustomed to doing in the past. I will never forget the day in court that I received a cupcake for my birthday, and I will never forget the kind, understanding words of wisdom from the judge, Mr. Rabble. Even though I was not doing well, I always appreciated and respected his ways of dealing with not only myself, but everyone else as well. His mindfulness stands out in my thoughts and so does the level of fairness and his messages of motivation that he shared with each of us. If ever there was a life coach for an addict, it would be him.

The number one thing that people can change is their thoughts, and as a result they can change their perspective, but sometimes we lie to ourselves about chance and we don't do anything to alter our environment. Having been released from the courtroom, I was then introduced to one of the alumni of the Program and driven to a local halfway house. I was grateful to be able to reside there, and I had known some of the staff from a previous stay at another halfway house. I was homeless and had needed the support and structure that would be available. The alumni that I had met earlier in the day had made it a point to drop by the halfway house and see how I was adapting. He had noticed that I had very little in the way of clothing, and to my surprise he returned later in the evening with two large bags of clothes. This act of kindness was very enlightening, and through this I experienced an unbelievable sense of gratitude and I learned a little bit about being humble and unselfish. I was further amazed to find out that this individual was not different than myself and was not a staff member or part of the team, as I first thought, but was a person that understood what I was going through because he himself was also a participant of the Drug Treatment Court Program.

With all these supports in place one would expect a seamless transition in respect to the challenges of abstinence, but for me there were many tears in the fabric of "my recovery plan," and the old saying of "a stitch in time may save many" is something that I am now able to reflect on with experience. I am once again serving another prison sentence, but incarceration hasn't tarnished the memories of the experience that I had while I was a participant in the London Drug Treatment Court Program. I remind myself that we change in gradual ways as we learn to adapt to life's challenges and that change is not an event but is a process, and a process that continues for as long as I can do.

Just recently I sent a letter to some of the members of the team, and even though I find myself sometimes wishing that things had been different and I had made better choices, I am not beating myself up today. And I can say that even though I have ended up back in prison, it doesn't mean that I did not benefit from my involvement in the program, because today I still believe in myself and I know there are still people out there that believe in me.

People can change. But beliefs about change matter a lot, and someone who wants to change has to believe that change is possible and "IT IS POSSIBLE."

Chris Dobson

Duty Counsel Lawyer, London Drug Treatment Court

Since a double measure of bitterness
Must follow the doing of your own will,
Do not do it.
Even though you remain in single bitterness,
Deny your desires and you will find what your heart longs for.
For how do you know any desire of yours is according to God?
St. John of the Cross (The Saying of Light and Love)

PEACE, LOVE, PARDON

FAITH, HOPE, LIGHT

JOY, CONSOLATION, UNDERSTANDING

FORGIVENESS

LOVE

GIVE

RECEIVE

LIFE

Prayer of The Dove (Reflections on St. Francis of Assisi)

As counsel for S., I knew prayer was an important part of his recovery. For graduation I wanted to give him a prayer that would challenge and encourage him. I chose the words of two great Saints for inspiration: St. John of the Cross, and St. Francis of Assisi. I also included a piece of art that I thought captured the "Spirit" of the words. As the picture I used was copyrighted it is not reproduced here. I have substituted a picture that I did following a retreat at Loyola House in Guelph, called "Rooted in Love" that captures that same Spirit of hope that I carry for S. and each of our participants whether they graduate or not. It is my belief, that our collective desire for the good of our participants has the power to heal them, either now or sometime later when they are ready to risk embracing a new reality of themselves as a loved person. I will continue to pray for the recovery of each of our participants. Their commitment to the hard work of recovery is also an inspiration to me.

☆

Kathy M.
Alumni, Toronto Drug Treatment Court

My Name is Kathy

My name is Kathy, I am fifty-two years old, and I have experienced problem use with crack cocaine.

I graduated from the Toronto Drug Treatment Court. I was admitted into the program by my own choice, because I wanted to end the destructive lifestyle of a crack addict.

To gain admittance to Drug Treatment Court, I plead guilty to trafficking of cocaine and possession of property obtained by crime.

This is my story.

I was born in Calgary, Alberta. I moved to Vancouver, B.C., where I lived until I was five years old. At that time my family moved to Toronto, where I still live. I am the middle child and was born into an upper-middle-class family. My father was an executive for a large corporation, which required him to travel away from home most of the time.

My problems began at a young age; my mother was mentally and physically abusive to me when my father was traveling. There was no abuse to my brother or sister. My father was always good to me when he was home; the abuse wasn't brought to his attention until I was twelve years old. By that time it was too late, the damage had already been done. Although I did well academically, my behaviour was disruptive. I got involved with a bad crowd and began using alcohol and drugs. I continued throughout my life making bad choices in relationships. All of my relationships were abusive.

I continued drinking and using drugs until I got pregnant with my son, then I quit and did not abuse drugs or alcohol until I was thirty-four years old. By then the mother of two children, I was also the assistant manager of a Toronto Dominion Bank branch. At this point, I got involved in a relationship with a man and he introduced me to cocaine. At first I was able to function and maintain my life and hide my crack cocaine problem.

After a few years I couldn't maintain my double life. My son was fifteen and my daughter was eight; my estranged husband allowed the children to live with him to make my life easier, the end result of that was the loss of my job, excessive drug use, and criminal activity. I became involved in a lot of crime, including the sex trade.

I was in and out of jail on a regular basis. When my behaviour would be noticed by friends and family, I would go to rehabilitation programs. I didn't do it for myself; I only went to keep others happy. I even had an earlier involvement with Judge Bentley and the Toronto Drug Treatment Court, but I ended up being expelled due to non-compliance and continued criminal activity.

I continued using drugs and having trouble with the police. I began to hang around with hardcore users and drug dealers. I kept on this path until I was arrested in November 2009. I stayed in jail for one month. I was going to proceed through the regular court system, but then I decided to apply for admittance to Toronto Drug Treatment Court. I was accepted.

For the first month, I continued using. Then I decided to give myself and the program a serious try. I was tired of the abusive relationships, being in and out of jails, and drug use. It was no longer enjoyable.

Since December 22, 2009, I have had only one drug use. This is the longest I have been clean in eleven years. I have been able to do this because of the help of Judge Bentley and the DTC staff and CAMH. I am now seeing professionals who can help me with my abuse issues.

I hope that with the continued support of Toronto Drug Treatment Court and CAMH I will be able to stay drug free.

Shane M.

Participant, Edmonton Drug Treatment Court

Excerpt from A *Warning From One Who Has Seen and Been Possessed...*

Yes the drug demons exist. They are Satan's top generals in charge of the ruin of souls. In this day and age, they are evil incarnated, tools of destruction using the illicit drugs of our time. Cocaine, crack speed, meth, heroin, ecstasy, and ice are all drugs manufactured and distributed to destroy lives. Breaking of souls is their result. Yes the result is only sadness and misery, families battered and broken, with innocence laid desolate and morals crippled and left decimated.

The drug demons exist – take warning, I've been personally rescued from their evil demonic power. I was lost over thirty years until God's saving grace saved me. Yet I am but only one of the very few that escape. For a divine purpose the heavens saved me and intervened. That is why I've written this — to bring light to this darkness.

The drug demons rise from the depths of hell to enslave those you love – your children or wife or parents – bringing darkness and insanity to them, leading them to the dark cursed death of the soul, a place worse than the ancient place called Sodom. Sodom was cursed for all eternity when the archangel Michael laid waste to both Sodom and Gomorrah so many years ago.

You only need to look around you and you can see great evil in this age and know that the Revelation of John while on the isle of Patmos is taking place in these times we are living in now. All hope seems to be lost for countless hundreds of thousands who are being controlled by demons. They walk down this path quickly and are tortured in preparation for Satan's abyss and his hell fires.

Even though these events are continuing without reprieve, there is hope for these people who are enslaved. They have brief moments of awareness of what is happening to them, and it is in these moments that goodness and light need to be there or within reach to bring compassion and mercy. Let the love of the faithful vanquish the demon's evil grasp upon these suffering souls.

There is an army of angels and saints ready to help do battle in the spiritual realm. We on this earthly place and time are to be the Lord's vessels of mercy and fortitude. We need to help our world, communities, homes, and families to stem the tide of destruction. We must act without delay, for soon the many will be left accursed and many of the chosen shall be laid waste for all eternity, never to see heaven. There is hope and success to be found at communities such as Sister Avira "conecollia" that rescue families and the addicts who once were being held by Satan's drugs and demons.

greetings: my name is Shane
I am a thankful participant in the
EDTCRC program.
Writing and drawing assists me in
expressing my deepest truths and understandings
it's a creative way in describing how my soul
interprets my thoughts and feelings
The past 37 years / life has been lost to me for
I was imprisoned by the relentless evil of addiction
So I pray you read what I've wrote seriously
in hopes you or someone you care for may
be enlightened, frightened to seek help or be
inspired spiritual truths usually have that effect
And for me the first day of my life was the day
I admitted I was an addict and was powerless and
needed help or I would surely die or be imprisoned.
Now 21 days from now on Dec 28th 2012 I will be
celebrating a year clean giving thanks to 12 steps
of NA ECA, AA to Slim Thorpe Recovery Center and
most importantly a special appriciation and thanks
to the EDTCRC program who made this my new clean
lawful, honest life in recovery posible. I truly believe
God has a purpose for me I trust that and I
now believe in miracles and prayers do get
answered.   Yours
                    sincerely,
                    Shane E.
                        michael mc donald

103

Trusting in the process
of recovery, living with
hope and being honest
with self and others
Learning to listen to share
and Believing prayers
are answered.
With a thankful heart
I humbly express my
gratitude to the Lord
and all the people who
with their honesty, love
mercy and compassion
enriched my life
in recovery.

Tears bring healing

Honesty Heals
and restores
Faith Hope
and Love.

Angela W.
Alumni, Durham Drug Treatment Court

Graduation Letter

To: Judge Rosenberg and Counsellors.
I would like to start this letter off with a big thank you to everyone in the Drug Treatment Program.

Thank you for all the help, all the support, all the encouragement, and the second chance at life. It means the world to me. I have come a very long way in the program, and because of this I have come so far in my life. I don't think I would have been able to, if I did not enter this program.

I literally had to take the steps I did in order to be the person I am today.

I am ready to graduate the program because of what I have accomplished.

I am on the right track and there is nothing but up from here.

I have accomplished all my goals that I had for myself, like getting clean, getting a job, and getting my own apartment. I have gotten to know myself and realize what a good person I am.

This program has shown me how to be one hundred percent honest, not only with everyone around me, but to be completely honest with myself.

That is the first step in my recovery.

It has been a huge thing in my life. I have accomplished all of my goals that I made for myself last year and have lived up to the court's expectations.

I will not let anyone down. This has been a life-changing experience.

You all should be very proud of what you do.

I remember when I first started this program, how big a mess I was.

But I always had high hopes and motivation, and even when times were tough I never gave up, and if I slipped I learned from it all. This program gave me lots of challenges, and thank God it did so I could succeed. This has defined me.

I can truly say, I am stronger than I have ever been. I know when I am done this program I will take everything I have learned with me; all the groups I have gone to have left such an impact on me, I love going to them and I plan to continue.

Before I started this program, my life was on a path of self-destruction...

Growing up was not easy, and to deal with pain I would numb it with drugs. I didn't believe I was worth anything, and when I was on my own with a bad addiction the only thing I thought of to do was to sell drugs, and that was so wrong.

Now I know how to live a clean, successful life.

I finally got my first job and it is such a great feeling. I am living an amazing life and I have a bright future ahead of me. My mind is so clear and positive, I am happy for the first time in my life. I owe it all to this program and all the people who worked with me.

I am so grateful for this blessing; I have faith in myself to keep moving forward and the knowledge to keep doing the good things I have learned in this program...

This honestly has given a second chance at a great life.

I am now a mature, honest, sober, and happy person.

Thank you for believing in me and for this opportunity. I hope you feel you can graduate me.

Thank you,
Angela White

P.S

This has been such a journey – my whole life has—and I have an incredible story and this story has a happy ending. I would love to move forward and help people that may have been through some of the same things I have, and if I could even just help one person by something I say, it would mean so much.

I will never surrender to drugs, and there really is a God somewhere.

Thanks again,
Angela White

Pamela J. Hill
Director, London Drug Treatment Court

Hope is the thing with feathers
That perches in the soul,
And sings the tune without the words,
And never stops at all...
- Emily Dickinson

I am a Drug Treatment Court professional.
I come to DTC, every time, with hope:
Hope that our team will find just the right balance of justice and mercy
for you

Hope that you will remember your best-self,
  or catch a glimpse of the person you want to be,
  discover the persistence, the inspiration, the courage
  and resources to pursue that self

Hope that our common humanity, yours and mine, will be recognized,
when our eyes meet
Hope for a transformation of you, of me, of our antiquated systems and
our vindictive society

Hope that smothers despair with its feathers
and cannot keep from singing, even when there are no simple words.

My hope is sustained by glimpses of your glory (veiled at times by drugs
and pain and anger and actions which obscure your best-self).

May feathered-hope occupy your soul and sing its own song ceaselessly.

Serena Coy

Former Therapist, Toronto Drug Treatment Court

The Journey of a Toronto Drug Treatment Court Alumna
(Excerpts from graduation speech for my client Paulette Walker)

The Beginning:

The Toronto Drug Treatment Court Program marked the first attempt at treatment that Paulette had made in the over twenty years of her addiction and criminal activity. One of the first questions she asked me when she began was, "When will I feel like a grown-up?" and my answer was, "When you begin to take responsibility for your life." With that simple answer, Paulette was off and running.

A Life in Progress:

She attended every group and individual session with few exceptions. She moved into Nazareth House to support her in her recovery. She attended additional groups to address other issues affecting her recovery; she took a computer course; and in spite of her fears, she reached out and began to connect with others and slowly learn to both love and trust herself.

The Graduation:
As a result, Paulette is here today with ten months drug and alcohol free. She is living on her own with her adult son, Roger. She is surrounded by family and others who love her, and she begins a food services training program in September. Paulette shared with me a few weeks ago that she finally feels like an adult.

The Community:
Many have supported Paulette on her journey and are here today to watch her transition into the next phase of the program... I would like to acknowledge the important role you have played, recovery is so much harder to do alone.

The Therapist:
Dear Paulette, it is an honour to have been a part of your recovery, to bear witness to your courage, determination, and your pain. Thanks for trusting me with this important job and all the best in your continued growth.

Life Today:
In August of 2003, Paulette graduated from the Toronto Drug Treatment Court. She immediately became an alumnus of the program and started her volunteer work with TITCH. Paulette went back to school and applied for a position as a Chef at the CAMH Russell Street cafeteria location, where she remained employed until July 2011.

In 2005, Paulette was invited as a guest of the United Nations to share her story and her thrill of being awarded that year's CAMH Courage to Come Back Award. In 2008 Paulette received the CAMH Edward Tremain Memorial Award of Excellence.

She was hired as the very first part-time Peer Support Worker in the Drug Treatment Program. While doing this meaningful work, she continued working part-time for Aramark in the Russell Street location. Paulette also decided she needed to go back to school, where she would be able to do her work more effectively.

Paulette continues working towards her education and she one day hopes to have her degree in Social Work. Paulette was recently hired as a full-time Peer Support Worker for the Toronto Drug Treatment Court Program.

The Journey continues...

S. Greene

Former Manager, Toronto Drug Treatment Court

Thank You

THANK YOU

EXCLAMATION

- a polite expression used when acknowledging a gift, service, or compliment, or accepting or refusing an offer.
- Example: thank you for your letter!, thank you for listening!, thanks for your help!

NOUN

- an instance or means of expressing thanks
- Example: Lucy planned a party as a thank you to the nurses, Shannon wrote this reflection as a thank you for her time in DTC

When first asked to write a reflection about my time in DTC, I was a bit puzzled about what to write, what to say. I'm by no means a writer, a poet, or even a storyteller!

Yes, there are LOTS of stories about my ten-plus years working in DTC, but what rings most true is the need to say THANK YOU.

I started work in DTC in May of 1999. I worked as a therapist, then as the Court Liaison Worker, then as Acting Manager, and then as Manager until early 2010.

My time in DTC makes up the bulk of my now-seventeen years at CAMH, and for that I'm very thankful.

THANK YOU to Mike Naymark for giving me the therapist job 'back in the day' and for your many years of wisdom about our clients and the work that we do. THANK YOU to my then clinical DTC colleagues: Bill, Anne, Miguel, Dave, Jill, Staci, Donna, Allison, Richard, Serena, Mair, Linda C, Linda W, Tanya, Tony, Raj, Tanya, Stephanie and Paulette.

Your hard work and commitment to the service and its clients made my work very rewarding.

THANK YOU to my then judicial DTC colleagues: Rose, Kofi, Illana, Kevin, Sandy, Andre, Barb, Joanne, John, Shellie, Darcy, Lizz, Annie, Catherine, Marilyn, Shelina, Will, Mel, Cameron, Margaret, Brent, Peter, Mary, and Maryka.

What a privilege it was to work closely with each of you over the years. Your willingness to balance the traditional standards of 'law & enforcement' with the influence of therapy, stages of change, and client engagement was inspiring and played a key role in my 'addiction to DTC' :)

THANK YOU to my then-Community DTC colleagues, there are FAR too many of you to list but a special thanks to Margaret, Brian, Wade, Deany, Evadne, Norm, Garvan, Carol, Azar, Jasmine, Greg, Laura, Tona, Shelley, Shari, Susan and Robin. Your support in getting the early foundations for housing, employment, and income assistance in place for clients was unwavering.

THANK YOU to the DTC clients. So many of you thank the team for helping you get out of jail, get housing, get reconnected to family, get treatment, get social support, get work, go back to school, get sober, get clean, get motivated, get your life back. BUT it is YOU that deserves the THANKS.

THANK YOU for showing up, THANK YOU for doing the work, THANK YOU for having the courage, THANK YOU for taking the risks, THANK YOU for putting yourself out there, THANK YOU for being honest, THANK YOU.

Last, but most importantly, THANK YOU to the Honourable Justice Paul Bentley.

THANK YOU for introducing me to the concept of restorative justice, and allowing us all to be part of this wonderful program. THANK YOU for your guidance over the years and for taking me under your wing! THANK YOU for allowing me to challenge you and to in turn be challenged. THANK YOU for enriching my experience with many international training opportunities and for allowing me to help spread the message of DTC worldwide.

THANK YOU for being a wonderful colleague, a trusted mentor, and a dearly loved friend.

You are very much missed.

THANK YOU

S. Greene

'I'
Participant, Toronto Drug Treatment Court

To Win Wars

Our war that we wage each day is met head-on by both sides.
The good side, the bad side.
Our future would be formulated here on the ground of heroism and signed with blood on our front lines.
Not in hollow conferences attended by those who don't rep themselves.
Our war is a war of life and death
We cannot indulge with those who are paper thin and masked up.
For some the cause is genuine, others it's just for the air of freedom.
To relearn the shit from our days of sandbox,
So we can STAND UP as men and women.
This war is real.
This war is long and hard.
There are more losses than victories in battle.
But not one loss loses the war.
I pray to my Father, whom art in heaven, for guidance and new ways of battle.
That's why I'm here, as a child, from days of sandbox.
To re-learn the techniques of this new form of battle
To take that, and win the war.

Thank you ALLAH for bringing me here
Thank you CAMH

☆

Joe E.
Alumni, Ottawa Drug Treatment Court

Just Another Day

I could be in jail tomorrow. Or the next day.

Which wouldn't be so bad. Considering.

I woke up just before dawn this morning. Shook the earwigs off of me and ran my fingers through hair that hadn't been washed in....I don't know how long. A few new spider bites, but all in all – no worse for the wear.

My current home is a PVC-coated canvas barbeque cover that I wrap myself in every night. Concealed in the bushes off of Island Park Drive, less than 250 metres from a street lined with two- to three-million dollar homes. Wouldn't the owners be pissed if they knew I was here.

And who I am.

Who I am. Not quite sure what that means anymore.

I am a booster. A professional thief. A con man.

Small time hoodlum. Big time crack addict. Somewhere between five hundred and a thousand dollars a day, big time crack addict. Which in turn, of course, means I am a pretty good booster. I generally am able to steal anywhere between five hundred and a thousand dollars per day of retail merchandise. On a good day I can get out with upwards of two thousand dollars, some of which I can return to the very store I stole it from for cash. Or at the very least, a gift card. Which I can easily sell.

Some of it I can turn directly into crack. My dealers all love a choice cut of beef, pork tenderloins, shrimp, and lobster. I, and many others, keep their freezers stocked. And they keep us loaded with crack.

Other items I can sell to a select few retailers who couldn't care less where their merchandise came from. One of my 'clients' has a store full of DVDs and Blu-Rays for sale to you – the average Joe – that were stolen by me – the below average Joe.

It isn't exactly a living. But I get by. Sort of.

Everything that you just read WAS true. For many years, I was that man, doing exactly those things. And, once in a while, getting caught and going to jail. Taking a break from the life, really. Jail is not as bad as you think it is. Nor is it as bad as I would tell you it was.

It sure as hell isn't as bad as the streets.

I woke up on the morning of July 18, 2006, in jail.

Again. And felt two things. One that I was used to. And one that I wasn't.

The first was fatigue. I was tired. Really, really tired. I had felt that before. I even had a cure. Crack.

The second was fear. That was something I was not used to. I had not felt fear in a very long time. I did not like the way it felt. What the hell was I afraid of? Certainly not the goons inside with me. I know them. I know what makes them tick. And talk. No, this was something different. It took me a little while to realize what it was. I was afraid of me. Of who, and what, I had become and was still becoming. I was afraid that the Joe I once was, many years ago, was about to be gone forever.

So I did something I had not done in a great many years. I asked for help. I reached out, through my lawyer, to the newly established Ottawa Drug Treatment Court and said that I need help with my drug addiction.

At the time I was not aware of it, but I needed help with so much more. Turns out my drug addiction wasn't my biggest problem. Nor was my criminal lifestyle. My biggest problem was me. And my lack of understanding of me. Or maybe, put more simply – my lack of me.

That is what the DTC Ottawa gave me. The opportunity to get to know and understand me. To take out the trash. And put in some value. To become me. Again. Someone I had not been since I was about nine or ten.

I am continuing daily, a little more than five years later, to learn about me. And to become the me that I will be today. And today, I can honestly say that I like that just fine.

Thank you, DTC Ottawa, and all of the wonderful people at Rideauwood.

CPSIA information can be obtained
at www.ICGtesting.com
Printed in the USA
LVIC06n1954091217
559183LV00001B/4

* 9 7 8 1 4 6 0 2 8 6 5 0 0 *